THE PHARISEES

AND OTHER ESSAYS

KANSAS SCHOOL OF RELIGION
University of Kansas
1300 Oread Avenue
LAWRENCE, KANSAS 66044

BM 175
. P4 B33

THE PHARISEES
AND OTHER ESSAYS

LEO BAECK

INTRODUCTION BY KRISTER STENDAHL

SCHOCKEN BOOKS · NEW YORK

TRANSLATED FROM THE GERMAN

First SCHOCKEN PAPERBACK *edition 1966*

Copyright © 1947, 1966 by Schocken Books Inc.

Library of Congress Catalog Card No. 66–15818

Manufactured in the United States of America

CONTENTS

LEO BAECK
(1873–1956)

Leo Baeck was looking for the essence of things. It is not surprising that the young rabbi in Oppeln, Germany, became known to a wider public by his sharp and extensive review[1] of Adolf Harnack's "The Essence of Christianity,"[2] and by his own subsequent study *The Essence of Judaism*.[3] Baeck's passionate critique of Harnack is more than understandable when one reads a passage like this one from Harnack's first lecture:

Jesus Christ's teaching will at once bring us by steps which, if few, will be great, to a height where its connexion with Judaism is seen to be only a loose one, and most of the threads leading from it into 'contemporary history' become of no importance at all.[4]

To Baeck such a statement displayed an incredible misunderstanding of Judaism, of Christianity, and of the history of Western culture. As he developed his thoughts about all three, he became an articulate spokesman for an era of continental Judaism in which what was worthwhile and lasting in Christianity and in Western Christendom was exactly its Jewish legacy, represented primarily by the Old Testament but also by the genuine teachings of Jesus as over against the ethical and theological escapism of the apostle Paul and his followers through the ages.

The clash between Baeck and Harnack was significant also because they shared many of the same presuppositions. They were equally bent upon discerning the "essence" of their religion. To both this enterprise had the same aims. Once the essence was properly extrapolated, it served as a liberating force. It became the standard by which inherited dogmatism could be dispensed with.

For Leo Baeck it belongs to the very essence of Judaism not to claim "the possession of what is fixed and final" ("Two World Views Compared," below, p. 133).[5] This is the claim of the Platonic tradition proper and as it became absorbed in the Christian tradition. "Its power consists in its ability to possess, dominate, and subject. It can be the consummated faith, the consummated dogma, the consummated state" (p. 144). In his essay Baeck describes Judaism in stark contrast to such a frame of mind. Judaism is the religion of tension. "In tension there is no possession. It cannot subject or dominate; it can only realize and re-create. . . . There is neither end nor conclusion to the reconciliation. . . . In it there is no permanent rest, but there is no death, either. . . ." (pp. 144f.). An openness toward the infinite belongs to the essence of Judaism. Consequently Paul goes wrong in "his longing after the absolute certainty of salvation" (p. 84).

Such an explication of the essence of Judaism has an obviously liberating force, and it supplies the deepest possible rationale for Baeck's relation to his own tradition. It makes it possible for him to perform an impressive apologetic task in a positive mood. The liberation goes deep enough to give his contribution that disarmingly positive character which Arthur Cohen catches when he says "Baeck exhibits Jewish life. He rarely argues it. Judaism is never a problem; but it is always a task."[6]

In Harnack the attention to the essence had similar effects, and he, like Baeck, found therein the device to steer a clear course between inherited orthodoxy and nihilistic positivism.[7] It is true that Harnack did not have the model of the open tradition, and he achieves his liberation rather by a drastic reduction to basic elements in the teaching and life of Jesus. But once the essence is defined, it sets him free to the same gallant work of apologetics, with the same double front: Orthodoxy on the one hand and nihilistic criticism on the other.

As Baeck pursues the Essence of Judaism, manifested in its history, his emphasis falls on ethics. Aesthetics and emotion, cult and ecstasy, always have negative connotations. His essay on "The Origin of Jewish Mysticism" (included in this volume) has one dominating tendency. It wants to show how "the specific feature of Jewish mysticism is precisely that it never ceases to be ethical" (p. 98). His quotes are mainly from the rabbinic passages in which we can see the attempts to domesticate the mythical tradition, and little attention is given to a positive understanding of that world which G. G. Scholem has opened up lately to a wider audience.[8]

This emphasis on ethics will strike the reader all through the following essays: The Synagogue versus the Temple in the history of the Pharisees; and—we are told—"in principle there was no place for ethics in Paul's system" (p. 79). It is coupled with the "democratic feature" in the Socratic tradition "that virtue and piety could be learned." For this same principle "characterizes Judaism. Here, too, we have the postulate that religion can be learned. It is the Torah, the 'teaching' " (p. 113).

We have singled out the concern for essence, and that for a specific reason. It is striking that nowhere in the essays that follow do we find a specific reference to food laws,[9] festivals, calendar, circumcision or Sabbath. The Law and the *Halakhah* are consistently treated as symbols for the ethical enterprise and its essential possibility. When once there is a reference to the Sabbath, it is in the context of Jewish Mysticism and its urge "to bring the beyond down to this earth, to transform the Sabbath, to whose poetry all its love is directed" (p. 105). When one reflects upon this beautiful expression, one sees that what the mystics achieved by their speculation and poetry, Baeck achieves by his emphasis on essence. The Sabbath and all other concrete commandments become symbols for the essence, be it of God as for mystics, or of Judaism as for Baeck. Not only cult and rite but also concrete commandments are absorbed in an image of Judaism as a "religion,"[10] a state of mind, an attitude toward reality. In this approach lies both the power and the weakness of the search for the essence and one could actually read Baeck's critique of the classical philosophical tradition (pp. 125-131) as a refutation of the search for a permanent essence.

But in his time Baeck has not felt that radical import of his emphasis on the historical nature of Judaism and its tradition. Under the pressure of the Western philosophical and Christian theological tradition he finds it self-evident that an essence of Judaism can be defined. Once defined, it can furthermore function as the timeless standard of truth within the

Jewish tradition. Thus Baeck participates in the dialogue between Judaism and Christianity on terms which are already set by the very traditions against which he argues. This makes for an easier discussion, but it leaves us with the uneasy feeling that something strange happens to the understanding of Judaism when it is so treated.

Who were the Pharisees? This question is of paramount significance to both Judaism and Christianity. It could be argued that it is of even greater significance for Christianity, since the teaching of Jesus and much early Christian material is available to us only in its sharp critique of and contrast to the Pharisees. Every misunderstanding of Pharisaism hence brings with it a misconception of the aims and intentions of early Christianity. It may well be that Baeck underestimates the drastic changes in Judaism caused by the events of 70 and 135 C.E., but even so, there is enough continuity between the Pharisaic sages and the Rabbis to make the question about the origin and actual tenets of the Pharisees in the time of Jesus a historical question which carries far less of a theological burden than does that question for the Christians.

That being so, Baeck's presentation of the Pharisees is of great interest for the dialogue between Judaism and Christianity and for Christian theology. In view of what we have said already, it is not surprising to find Baeck in favor of the most positive alternative as to the origin of the term Pharisee.[11] He chooses what could be called the Sifra line of etymology: In Sifra to Lev. 19:2 the Midrash renders the phrase "You shall be holy" as "You shall be *perushim*, i.e. separated" (p. 5), and Baeck is anxious to retain this positive connotation of "holy community" as the essential one in his presentation of the Pharisees. Thus he gives significant attention to how this community liberates Judaism from the priestly, the cultic, and the Temple. He shows how the Torah assumes a new centrality through authoritative interpretation. He sees how the eschatological messianism and the wisdom tradition "endowed both their isolation and their interpretation of the Scriptures with a tendency towards the infinite and universal" (pp. 28f.). Baeck is, of course, not blind to the grave faults of many a follower of Pharisaism—"often because of the character of Pharisaism itself" (p. 49)—but once more he refers to the "essence"; he returns to the Sifra quotation and speaks of it as a "heroic effort to prepare the ground for the kingdom of God" (p. 50).

The second essay in the following selection is a part of a longer article first published in Germany in 1938: "The Gospel as a Document of the History of the Jewish Faith."[12] In the complete essay Baeck demonstrates the Jewishness of Jesus and the gospels. This does not only refer to Jesus as the teacher but also as the one in whom his followers saw Hosea's prophecy fulfilled "raised up on the third day" (Hos. 6:2).[13] And the gospel is "a book—and certainly not a minor work— within Jewish literature . . . not because, or not only because, it contains sentences which also appear in the same or a similar form in the Jewish works of that time. . . . Rather it is a Jewish book because—by all means and entirely because— the pure air of which it is full and which it breathes is that of the Holy Scriptures; because a Jewish spirit, and none other, lives in it; because Jewish faith and Jewish hope, Jewish suffering and Jewish distress, Jewish knowledge and

xii

Jewish expectations, and these alone, resound through it—a Jewish book in the midst of Jewish books."[14] Baeck then proceeds by giving a synoptic reconstruction of the gospel material—the events from John the Baptist to the resurrection, and the sayings and parables.[15] These he presents as that Jewish book.

The section included in this selection deals from a Jewish point of view with what has become one of the decisive features of contemporary biblical studies as represented by form-criticism[16] and the study of transmission.[17] It is a contribution to that enterprise.[18]

But the break with Judaism came with Paul. In "Judaism in the Church" we have a classical example of a powerful model of Jewish interpretation of the New Testament and subsequent church history. The essay is parallel to the more elaborate study of Christianity as the "romantic religion" versus Judaism as "classical."[19] It is built on the basic axioms of 19th century Protestant, especially German, scholarship,[20] with its dichotomy between the teaching of Jesus and the theology of Paul. Paul is now the creator of the Christian Church, and the history of the Church and the West is seen under the Lutheran pattern of Law and Gospel, now interpreted as ethical realism[21] versus the escapism of faith, certainty of salvation and sacramental assurance. And while the tension between these two elements, between Judaism and what Baeck here calls Paulinism, has had its long and complex history, it looks to Baeck as if "Judaism" is winning out in most of the forms of modern Protestantism.

Already when Baeck expressed these sentiments and hopes the theological climate of Protestantism had changed substantially. Ethical monotheism of the kind Baeck and Harnack took for granted was no longer the reasonable core of religion and culture. In the 19th century there had been a more radical challenge to theology than the one which shook the thinking of Baeck and Harnack. Already in 1841, Feuerbach had written his book on *The Essence of Christianity* in which theology was ruthlessly reduced to anthropology. It is significant that men like Barth felt this radical challenge as the decisive one and could not find satisfaction in the mild liberalism of Harnack.[22] At the same time the school of History of Religion did its utmost to smash the attractive images of Jesus and the best of his followers and contemporaries as reasonable men with exactly those ethical ideals which we like most. Johannes Weiss and Albert Schweitzer widened the gap between the eschatological abstrusities of Jesus and modern man. What had been called the essence of Christianity now appeared to have been a highly apologetic abstraction without any serious historical attention to what Jesus or Paul or John had considered essential in their work and message.

The more radical critique of religion and the irresistible impact of a more realistic historical picture of the period of Christian beginnings are the necessary presuppositions for Protestant theology after World War I. Barthianism, Neo-orthodoxy, de-mythologizing and now the Honest-to-God debate with its experiments in religionless Christianity make the intellectual climate of men like Harnack and Baeck look rather mild, and the problematic appears serene and elevated.

In an article from 1952 Baeck returned to a question crucial to his whole model of Jewish and Christian history: The Faith of Paul.[23] It is impressive to note the differences between this presentation and the analysis which formed the basis for Baeck's model of the romantic Christianity versus the classical Judaism. Baeck had always seen a tension in Paul between a Jewish heritage and an antinomian faith, but in 1952 the accents have changed considerably, and he is anxious to show how Paul even in his mission to the Gentiles is within the Jewish faith, and how his theology is dominated by Jewish problems, treated and solved in the Jewish type of scriptural interpretation by analogy. One can read Baeck's interpretation of Paul from the 1950's in different ways. Reinhold Mayer, in his extensive study of *Christianity and Judaism as seen by Leo Baeck*, considers it a drastic reversal in Baeck's scholarship and intimates that thereby the foundation of Baeck's model of Judaism and Christianity has been demolished.[24] While it is true that Paul's role in that model has changed quite substantially, the model itself may well remain suggestive and helpful. Many scholars would see Paul in Corinth exactly as the critic of the spiritualistic escapism and enthusiasm of those who claimed to have attained more of the consummation than was actually to be had. Paul is thus the first of the critics of "Christian romanticism" when he stresses that the Christian lives still in the world of work (II Thess. 3:6-12), suffering (Rom. 8:18-25) and death. The enthusiasts are those who claim wrongly that "the resurrection has already happened" (II Tim. 2:18).

What strikes me in Baeck's revised portrait of Paul's faith is rather something else. Baeck has been sensitive to the impetus of the school of History of Religion which freed Pauline studies from the patterns supplied by liberal and orthodox theology. He has been—at least temporarily—liberated from the concern for essence, congenial to such systematic abstractions. One could, of course, say that he now just extends even to Paul his program of reclaiming Judaism in Christianity. But there is more to it, for here he is able to recognize as essentially Jewish what must at the same time still appear utterly alien to his own Jewish faith, i.e. to what he liked to call the essence of Judaism.

Most of what Baeck wrote—and all the essays here published—have Christianity as a partner in the dialogue. It is not only to the Christian they have the tone of *audiatur et altera pars,* but for him they are an especially welcome voice. The Jewish voice is badly needed, and when we have phrased our introduction in critical terms we have done so since we are afraid that that voice was not always free enough from the imposition of the presuppositions of a dominating, so-called Christian culture. The rules of the debate were set by the other party—not in the obnoxious manner of the medieval and 16th century debates, but in a more subtle fashion, within the cultural confines of continental Europe at the turn of the century.

Nevertheless Baeck's voice is often beautifully clear and distinct and his mind and sensitivities are informed by the riches of his tradition. It is interesting to note that many of the things he stresses have taken on significance also for Christians during these last decades. They are not always the features he saw as areas of growing agreement. They are rather those elements which to him were the marks of demarcation.

As a teacher of Midrash he is forceful in his emphasis on the need for continuous interpretation of the Scriptures. Both at Vatican II and in Protestantism new reflection on the relation between scripture and tradition has opened up new avenues of understanding. It will no doubt do the same in the dialogue between Judaism and Christianity. The recognized need for interpretation actually implies that *both* are historical communities rather than fixed systems of thought. To both the Bible speaks only as it is interpreted. In its enthusiasm over this new, yet old insight a commission of the World Council of Churches went as far as to suggest that the Church lives not so much *sola scriptura* but *sola traditione*.

One reads with much interest Baeck's observations on the Torah versus Gnosis. The former is possible to teach and hence it needs the preacher; the latter needs rather the herald (p. 113). These words have an ominous ring to students of contemporary Christian theology. The message of the herald, the *kerygma*, has for forty years been the slogan by which one tries to understand the nature of the Christian message, the intention of the Gospel, the existential dimension of the faith. It may well be that Baeck here points toward a basic difference between Judaism and Christianity, and many Christians would say so; but is that necessarily so? Both communities depend ultimately on God's gracious act and election. God's heralds were not unknown to Abraham or Moses. And the teaching and "educational" preaching has its role also in the community called by baptism and sustained by the Manna of the Eucharist.

While Baeck's emphasis is strongest on ethics, he is certainly aware of the promise of and the longing for the Kingdom, The Age to Come. His critique of romantic Christianity is actually a critique of a peculiar interpretation of Jewish eschatology. In the essays to follow this eschatological element in Judaism is constantly present. When he described Judaism over against the Greek world of philosophy and mystery cults, it was exactly this eschatology which gave him the decisive lever. It is by eschatology that Judaism remains the religion of tension, freed from the dead grip of "finality" (pp. 144f.).

It would appear—as it often does to Baeck—as if Christianity were always on the side of fulfilled and realized eschatology. And it is true, that when Christian theology became translated into the categories of Greek philosophy it lost much of its original eschatological tension. But in the New Testament and beyond there is that same tension for which we just saw Paul fighting with the enthusiasts in Corinth. In one of the earliest prayers at the Eucharist the Church cries: *Marana tha*, Lord come! (Didache, cf. I Cor. 16:22; Rev. 22:20).[25]

In his introduction to Baeck's essays on Judaism and Christianity Walter Kaufmann presents Baeck as one who did not only defend Judaism as not inferior to Christianity but rather as distinctly superior.[26] It should be noted, however, that Baeck does so as a wise father who sees how his own children have wandered astray. For to him there is always enough of Judaism in Christianity so that he can recognize the church as the child of Judaism. To me this is not arrogance, but love. And once we free ourselves from the alien and superimposed concept of "religion" we cannot only see and feel this, but we can perhaps find a conceptual framework where the dialogue can become both deeper and sharper. For we are two communities which are related to each other in a most peculiar

xviii

way. The church is the supplicant here. The church is the one who must give reason for her arrogant claim to the Scriptures and the Promises, to the Kingdom and the Messiah. She tries to do so in Jesus' name—to give those traditional words their full weight. The Christian is the prodigal son who hopes that our older brother will not be angry with him, but that they will meet together at the banquet.

KRISTER STENDAHL

Harvard Divinity School
September, 1965

NOTES

1. "Harnacks Vorlesungen über das Wesen des Christenthums," *MGWJ* 45(1901), pp. 97-120.
2. *Das Wesen des Christenthums* (1900); in its English translation Harnack's work received the title *What is Christianity?* (1900; paperback edition with an introduction by R. Bultmann, New York, 1957).
3. *Das Wesen des Judentums* (1905, 1922,² 1932⁶); English translation, *The Essence of Judaism* (London, 1936, rev. ed., New York, 1948).
4. *What is Christianity?*, p. 16.
5. Cf. Leo Baeck, "Hat das überlieferte Judentum Dogmen?," in *Aus drei Jahrtausenden* (1938, 1958²), pp. 12-27.
6. Arthur A. Cohen, *The Natural and the Supernatural Jew* (New York, 1962), p. 109, in the chapter on "The German Jewish Renaissance," where Cohen singles out H. Cohen, L. Baeck, F. Rosenzweig and M. Buber for detailed analysis.
7. *See below*, p. 131, where Baeck explains the organic relation between these two enemies: The closed and perfect system and "the universal nihilism—political, ethical, and spiritual—[which] always has its inception in the idea of finality."

8. Gershom G. Scholem, *Major Trends in Jewish Mysticism* (New York, 1954, paperback ed., 1961).

9. *See also* Baeck's article "Speisegebote" in the 2nd ed. of *Die Religion in Geschichte und Gegenwart,* vol. V (1931), 678f.; cf. his article "Gesetz," *ibid.,* vol. II (1928), pp. 1127-29.

10. For a penetrating critique of the impact of the term "religion," *see* Wilfred C. Smith, *The Meaning and End of Religion* (New York, 1962) ; cf. *Harvard Theological Review* 58 (1965), pp. 432-51.

11. Cf. L. Finkelstein, *The Pharisees and the Men of the Great Synagogue* [Texts and Studies of the Jewish Theological Seminary of America 15] (1950/5710), p. xiv: "The evidence seems conclusive that the word, *perushim,* actually means heretics, and was used in that sense very frequently in the Mishna." According to Finkelstein it was originally a derogatory term, which the Pharisees accepted and gave glory. For a discussion of the different alternatives *see* M. Black's article "Pharisees" in *The Interpreter's Dictionary of the Bible* II (1962), p. 776.

12. The full article is included in *Judaism and Christianity: Essays by Leo Baeck,* translated with an introduction by Walter Kaufmann (Philadelphia, 1958/5719), pp. 45-62.

13. *Ibid.,* p. 100.

14. *Ibid.,* pp. 101f.

15. *Ibid.,* pp. 102-36.

16. On form criticism *see,* e.g., R. Bultmann and K. Kundsin, *Form Criticism* (1934).

17. On transmission *see* B. Gerhardsson, *Memory and Manuscript: Oral Tradition and Written Transmission in Rabbinic Judaism and Early Christianity* (Uppsala, 1961).

18. This kind of study, and Baeck's attitude in this matter is especially impressive when compared with the almost vulgar recent treatment of the gospels by Dagobert D. Runes, *The Jew and the Cross* (New York, 1965), where we hear about gospel material "as presented to us by the scribes of the Bishop of Rome" (p. 26), or even "the Scriptures as set down by the evangelists of the Bishop of Rome in the fourth century" (p. 25). While Runes speaks out of justifiable indignation, his disregard for

historical data and his attempts to find a scapegoat (the Pope) are helpful to nobody.

19. *See* Kaufmann ed., pp. 189-292.

20. *See* the extensive study by Gösta Lindeskog, *Die Jesusfrage im neuzeitlichen Judentum*. Ein Beitrag zur Geschichte der Leben-Jesu-Forschung (Uppsala, 1938).

21. This positive connotation of "Law" dominates the material in the significant trilogy *Judaism and Christianity* (New York, 1937-38), edited by W. O. E. Oesterley [Vol. I, *The Age of Transition*], H. Loewe [Vol. II, *The Contact of Pharisaism with other Cultures*], and E. I. J. Rosenthal [Vol. III, *Law and Religion*].

22. *See* Barth's introduction to L. Feuerbach, *The Essence of Christianity*, included in the Harper Torchbook ed. (1957). *See also* J. Glasse, "Barth on Feuerbach," *Harvard Theological Review* 57(1964), pp. 69-96, and M. Vogel, "The Barth-Feuerbach Confrontation," *ibid.*, 59(1966).

23. "The Faith of Paul," Journal of Jewish Studies 3 (1952), pp. 93-110. Now in ed. Kaufmann, pp. 139-68.

24. Reinhold Mayer, *Christentum und Judentum in der Schau Leo Baecks* [*Studia Delitzschiana* 6] (1961), pp. 105f.; cf. pp. 58-64.

25. On this and on the dialogue between Judaism and Christianity *see* my essay: "Judaism and Christianity: Then and Now," *New Theology No. 2*, ed. M. E. Marty and D. G. Peerman, (New York, 1965), pp. 153-64.

26. *Op. cit.*, p. 6.

PREFACE TO THE FIRST EDITION

Leo Baeck is a representative figure of European Jewry. At one time the leading rabbi in Berlin and a faculty member of the Academy for the Study of Judaism (*Hochschule für die Wissenschaft des Judentums*), he won scholastic renown for his classical studies, his work in the history of Jewish thought, and his studies in early Christianity.

The great turning point in Baeck's life occurred in 1933, when he was sixty years old.

The events set in motion in this year drowned German Jewry in a chaos of lawlessness. Baeck was called to the presidency of the council created to represent the Jewish community of Germany (*Reichsvertretung der deutschen Juden*), and served in effect as the spokesman of German Jewry. In this difficult and exposed position he was nevertheless able—in defiance of the constant threat of the concentration camp—by his presence to radiate hope and confidence.

The pogrom of November 9, 1938, the burning of the synagogues, and the arrest of all prominent German Jews clearly indicated what was in store for the Jew in Germany. Baeck, despite invitations from congregations and learned institutions all over the world, remained in Germany with the poor, old, and sick of his people.

In January 1943, together with thousands of other Jews, he was transported to the concentration camp in Theresienstadt. Baeck survived, purely by an accident.

In Theresienstadt, despite the degrading circumstances, groups of people came together and were able to improvise an intellectual life. This partial conquest of misery and humiliation was the result of the presence of Leo Baeck. In what Baeck called the "hours of freedom," he gave instruction—without books, there were none to be had—in the world's great documents: the Bible, Plato's dialogues, the works of Aristotle, Spinoza, Locke, Hume, and Kant, as well as the living Jewish classics: the talmudic Aggadah, Maimonides, Yehudah ha-Levi. This was his answer to that world which marshaled so much power and ingenuity to strip those sent to the concentration camps of their humanity. Baeck, the quiet teacher, became a symbol of the free man and of the superiority of the human spirit over slavery.

In May 1945, Theresienstadt was freed by Allied troops. Baeck, seventy-two years old, emerged from it erect and strong of will. He had realized in practice the high principles that he had interpreted during more than forty years of scholarly work.

His first work, *The Essence of Judaism* (*Das Wesen des Judentums,* 1905), is the most important liberal exposition of Judaism. It was translated into many languages; into English in 1936. In 1933 a collection of essays was issued under the title of "Paths in Judaism" (*Wege im Judentum*, Schocken Verlag, Berlin). The edition of his second volume of essays, "Out of Three Thousand Years" (*Aus Drei Jahrtausenden*), printed in 1938, was destroyed by the Gestapo.

Some of these essays appear in this volume. Beneath the variety of subjects Baeck considers—Pharisaism, Jewish and Greek sermonology, the origin of Jewish mysticism, the influence of Jewish ideas in the church, etc.—there goes on the perennial discussion between Christian and Jew. These essays have an added importance in a time such as ours, when this discussion ordinarily alternates between the extremes of shallow eclecticism and aggressive dogmatism.

Baeck, the historian, is devoted to the past; the spiritual leader is concerned with the present—but his gaze is fixed on the future. "Perhaps," he once said, "a human being does not die until he no longer sees anything but the past and the present moment."

THE PHARISEES

THE PHARISEES

Since ancient times the term "Pharisees" has been much used but little understood. In order to penetrate a significant portion of Jewish religious history, however, and in particular the period that alone casts light on the origins of Christianity, it is of crucial importance that this name and the role of the men who bore it be correctly comprehended.

The problem has been investigated repeatedly during the last century. Its purely linguistic aspects are unmistakable and clear; the word "Pharisee," which is derived from the Greek rendition of the Hebrew word *Parush*, or the Aramaic *Perishaya*, means "separated" and "isolated." But at this point the real difficulties begin; for, like every verb, the one from which this term is derived can denote a multiplicity of relationships. From what and by what means were these people isolated or separated, and why and when? A wealth of answers has been given to these questions.

In the biblical Books of Ezra and Nehemiah, the story is told of those who returned from the Babylonian Exile, and it is said of the best among them that they "had *separated* themselves (*Nivdalim*) unto them from the filthiness of the nations of the land" (Ezra 6:21). At one time it was thought that the origin and meaning of our term were to be found here. In the Books of the Maccabees, which portray the conflict between Greek and

Jewish thought and life, it is related how the "devout" separated themselves from those whose Judaism was less strict than their own. Attempts have been made to connect the term "Pharisee," both as to its meaning and the time of its origin, with this reference. Still others think it arose out of the political struggles that caused so many dissensions among the Jewish people under the Maccabean kings, and try to derive the concept of "isolation" from these struggles. And, finally, there is a difference of opinion as to whether the name was first chosen by those who bore it or was first given them by their adversaries.

If no satisfactory answer to our questions was found in the past—and, as we have said, such an answer is the key to the understanding of a significant period—the chief reason for this lay in the failure to recognize or consider all the historical sources in which the decisive facts and relationships are revealed. True, the above-mentioned biblical and post-biblical books were studied in detail. Then Flavius Josephus was painstakingly examined; in his two great works, *Antiquities of the Jews*, a history of Israel to the time of the great insurrection against Rome, and the *History of the Jewish War*, devoted to that insurrection (from 66 to 70 C.E.), there is a detailed account of the Pharisees, as well as of the Sadducees, their adversaries, and the Essenes, their spiritual cousins. Likewise, the passages of the New Testament in which the Pharisees are mentioned were cited, and finally passages from the Mishnah and its supplement, the Tosefta, the first books to follow the Bible and its tradition of the laws. But the tannaitic Midrashim— that is, the biblical interpretations and homiletic commentaries of the Tannaim, the first generations of the teachers of the law —were more or less disregarded. And yet these commentaries, whose truth in this connection is confirmed by passages from other expositions of the Haggadah—the old explanation and exegesis of the Scriptures—are of crucial importance for the study of the ideas and language of the period because of the reliability of their tradition. And they point a clear path towards an understanding of the term "Pharisee."

In Sifra, the old Midrash of the Akiba school to Leviticus, which supplies us with material that is in part as old or older than Josephus' work, the word *Parush*, "separated," is given as an explanatory translation of the biblical word *Kadosh*, "holy." The well-known sentence, "Ye shall be holy," is thus translated as "Ye shall be *Perushim*." [1] This new word is also used where the holiness of God is expressed. God is quoted as saying: "Just as I am *Parush*, so ye shall be *Perushim*." [2] These sentences are transmitted without mention of their author; they are anonymous Haggadah, and as a rule this points to an early origin. They show unmistakably that our word *Perushim* at that time expressed the attribute of holiness and the moral summons to it. Hence it might have become the name of a community of Jews, a name that in their minds, or as applied to them—the possibility that it was first used ironically by enemies is not excluded—denoted a personal and national ideal of the saint, and in which they saw contained the meaning of their community and the goal of their movement.

If the quality referred to by the word *Perushim* is thus used to denote the quality of "holiness," it falls into a definite historical context. For the term "the saints" was used from Maccabean times on as a term of honor for the "community" of Judaism. In the Book of Daniel this word, which heretofore, even in the Book of Zechariah and the Wisdom of Joshua ben Sirach, as well as in earlier passages of Daniel itself, had

5

denoted the heavenly hosts, was applied in a laudatory sense to the community of those Jews who had remained faithful to their God. It retained this meaning in the subsequent period, as proved by passages from the First Maccabees, the Book of Tobit, and the Wisdom of Solomon. In the writings of the New Testament, especially in the epistles of Paul, this word became the name of the Christian community in conformity with the tendency of a new community to appropriate the honorific titles of the old. As for its meaning, it is in all these passages equivalent to the word "community," *ecclesia*; for instance, the phrase in the story of Peter's miracle with Tabitha, "he had called the saints" (Acts 10:41), really means "he had called the community." The "saints" are the "community," the *ecclesia*, which was opposed to the "nations," or the heathen, as early as in the Book of Sirach.

Saintliness, the characteristic of the *Perushim* or "community," actually appears as such an opposition in the ancient texts. Here it means separateness from the nations, and in this connotation it has an inner association with the term *Nivdalim* as used in the Books of Ezra and Nehemiah. In the First Maccabees this separateness is seen as the principle of the "community," and its adversaries regard it as the source of all evil: "In those days there came forth out of Israel lawless men and persuaded many saying, 'Let us go and make a covenant with the nations that are round about us, for ever since the time we became separated from them, many misfortunes have overtaken us.' "

The same idea is found in the tannaitic Midrashim; here, too, this separation, which gives its name to the *Perushim*, is a separation from the "nations." Thus the Mekhilta, a rabbinical commentary on Exodus, of the school of Rabbi Ismael,

6

the friend and theoretical opponent of Rabbi Akiba, explains the sentence, "Ye shall be unto me a kingdom of priests and a holy nation," as follows: "Holy and sanctified, that is to say, separated, *Perushim*, from the nations and their abominations." [3] Likewise, in Sifra, the commandment, "Ye shall sanctify yourself and be holy," is explained as follows: "This means first of all the sanctification that consists in separation from the heathens." [4] In the same work, the sentence, "Just as I am *Parush*, ye shall be *Perushim*," which we have mentioned above, is followed by, "If ye are separated from the nations, says the Lord, ye belong to me; if not, ye belong to Nebuchadnezzar, the king of Babylon, and his companions." [5] A similar idea is expressed in the Mekhilta of Simeon ben Yohai, the disciple of Akiba: "Only if ye separate yourselves from the nations are ye mine." [6]

It is needless to say that even at that time the notion of exclusiveness was not the sole content of the idea of saintliness; the negative determination was always accompanied by a positive one. Thus, in the Sifra, we find that the passage, " 'Ye shall sanctify yourselves and be holy'—this means first of all the sanctification that consists in separation from the heathens," is immediately followed by this passage, " 'Ye shall be holy'—this means the sanctification that consists in practising all the commandments." [7] Likewise, in the Sifre, the tannaitic Midrash on Numbers and Deuteronomy, we read: " 'Ye shall be holy unto your God'—this means sanctification through the practice of all the commandments." [8] And again, in an expanded form, we read in Rabbi Simeon's Mekhilta: " 'Ye are a holy nation unto the Lord, your God'; and by this is meant sanctification through the commandments; for when God gives Israel a new commandment, he gives it further sanctification." [9] But there is a difference between the quality demanded of the individual by this use of the word "holy" and the clearly defined title that the same word was used to bestow. In the latter use the word was applied to the community, and it meant above all that other duty, separation from the nations. Through this the community became a community of "saints," of *Perushim,* and thus a "community" in the full sense.

Thus we find that the term "Pharisee" means what at that time was for the "community" of Judaism the ordinance of its self-preservation: the sainthood of exclusiveness, and this exclusiveness was with regard to the "nations." Essentially, as a moral summons and a task, its meaning is the same as that contained in the historic fact of the idea of election. However, it seems that still another element is present in the word. The commandment of separation and the saintliness defined by it applies fundamentally to all the Jews, including the Diaspora; thus Josephus speaks approvingly of the fact that the Diadochi, the successors to Alexander the Great, assigned a separate city quarter to the Jews of Alexandria "to enable them to follow their way of life more purely, since the non-Jews would then mix with them less." [10] However, the region in which the most thoroughgoing separation occurred at that time was nevertheless supposed to be Palestine, the Holy Land. Saintliness was attributed pre-eminently to its regions, and all the prescriptions mentioned above applied to it with even greater strictness.

In this context an old tradition acquires its full meaning: "Jose ben Yoezer of Tzeredah and Jose ben Yohanan of Jerusalem ordained that the land of the nations be considered levitically impure." [11] And in the name of Jose ben Halafta, the

8

father of the Jewish chronology, his son Ismael, a younger contemporary of Akiba, makes the same statement, although he gives a different date: "Eighty years before the destruction of the Temple it was ordained that the land of the nations be considered levitically impure." [12] Even though there is a contradiction between the two dates, for the men mentioned in the former passage are named in the Sayings of the Fathers among the old Soferim, the Scribes, and thus must have lived about a century and a half before the date mentioned in the latter passage, the content of the tradition is clearly established. It, too, shows us the Holy Land as the real goal and sphere of the separation, so that the true Pharisees may be assumed to have been the communities of Palestine. This is in harmony with the fact that both Josephus and the New Testament mention the Pharisees only where Palestinian Jews are concerned.

In connection with the foregoing an explanation may be found for a term dating from an earlier time, which is preserved in the talmudic literature. Old traditions are here sometimes ascribed to the "holy community in Jerusalem." [13] Later talmudic teachers sought to interpret this epithet, but did not really explain it. It will possibly become clear if we assume that within Palestine, the domain of saintliness, Jerusalem was considered a narrower, more circumscribed domain of "saintliness" or "separation," and that the "community" of Jerusalem was accordingly considered *the* "holy community" in this narrower sense. This is in accord with the meaning of the term "the saints" as used in the New Testament. Here the word has a twofold meaning: first, the comprehensive meaning by which, as we have shown before, all the Christian communities are meant; and second, as in Paul, a restricted meaning that refers only to the Christian community of Jerusalem.

It is possible, however, to construe the sentences in which it occurs in the restricted sense as applying to all the Christian communities of Palestine, so that here, too, the inhabitants of the Holy Land, just as was the case with the Pharisees, are called the "saints" in the special meaning of the term.

Thus the term "Pharisee" becomes more explicit. And when it is related to the tradition mentioned above, according to which the lands of the nations were considered levitically impure, its historical meaning can also be defined more clearly, especially if the duality of this tradition is traced back to a double event, namely, that the decree concerning the lands of the nations was issued twice. It was issued for the first time by Jose ben Yoezer and Jose ben Yohanan, that is to say, at a time when the policy of the Hasmonean princes began to look beyond the borders of Palestine. This accords with the fact that Josephus mentions the Pharisees for the first time when discussing the period of Jonathan, the Hasmonean prince, and again—a fact also confirmed in its essentials by a talmudic tradition—when discussing the period of John Hyrcanus, the second ruler after Jonathan. Moreover, an explicit time reference in the Palestinian Talmud places these two teachers, Jose ben Yoezer and Jose ben Yohanan, in that same period. At that time, because of the territorial extension of the Jewish state, and perhaps also because of the hiring of a mercenary army, the question of separation from "the nations" became an urgent one. Thus it fits well with our interpretation that Josephus mentions the Pharisees once more when speaking of the period of Herod, that is to say, the period when for the second time, eighty years before the destruction of the Temple, the lands of the nations were declared to be impure. At this time, too, the geographical expansion of the country made the question of "the separateness" a matter of concern. And for that reason it is again no accident that Josephus' last mention of the Pharisees occurs in the passage of his history that deals with the transformation of the Jewish land into a Roman province—an event that made that same question especially acute.

Thus we infer that Pharisaism was originally a movement aimed at separation from the nations and at saintliness to be achieved by this means; it appeared originally and reappeared when the policies or destinies of the land seemed to be following an opposite path. It arose for the same reasons as the movement of the Hasidim, the Asidaeans or the "Devout," mentioned in the Books of the Maccabees. But whereas the Maccabees took up arms in defense of freedom of religion, imperilled by a foreign ruler and his Jewish allies, Pharisaism was directed against an encroachment upon the ideal of the Jewish community. The religion itself was no longer in danger, neither in the period of the last Hasmonean princes, nor of Herod, nor of the Roman procurators. The goal of the Pharisees' struggle was the preservation of the strict purity and cohesion of the Jewish community; their task was to erect and defend the *Seyag la-Torah*, the protective fence around the religion. And when the Pharisees set out to expound the history of their tradition, they were not wrong to place this crucial task at the very beginning. "Moses received the Torah on Mount Sinai and handed it down to Joshua; Joshua to the elders; the elders to the prophets; and the prophets handed it down to the men of the Great Assembly. These latter said three things: Be deliberate in judgment, raise up many disciples, and make a fence around the Torah—*Seyag la-Torah!*" [14]

The Pharisees were thus not a party, as so often asserted by modern historians, or yet a school or a sect, as Josephus says,

to please his Greek and Roman readers—although every movement has some trace in it of the party and the school—but a
movement within the Jewish people. This sheds light on the
name they bore, *Perushim,* as well as on the various activities
in which they engaged. They were able, and perhaps were
sometimes compelled, as in the times of King Alexander
Jannaeus, and later under the Roman governors, to become
zealots who tried to enforce their separation by violence. They
were able, and were sometimes compelled, in times of disaster,
to become ascetics who strove to maintain their exclusiveness
through the effort of renunciation. They were able, and later
were compelled, to become Essenes, who sought through isolation to become completely separated.

In addition to the problem of the name, there is the problem
of the position of the Pharisees within the nation as a whole.
Here, too, we have two sources of information: the testimony of
Josephus and that of the Tannaim. The passages of the Gospels
that refer to the Pharisees have no historical significance; in
them our term is not used in its historical connotation but only
serves the purposes of ridicule and deprecation. They refer
not to "saints" but to hypocrites, not to the pious but to the
sanctimonious. And even in the case of Josephus, the audience
for which he wrote must be taken into account. Because his
purpose was to describe to educated and philosophically-
minded Romans and Greeks the various tendencies active in
the Jewish people, he tried to make them more intelligible or
more interesting by locating these tendencies within a general
philosophic context that led to those very questions that preoccupied his readers. If we are to recognize the Pharisees
whom he describes, they must be divested of the philosophical
cloak he wrapped about them. Similar reservations must be

made with regard to the talmudic passages. In the Talmud the *Halakhah* aspect, the aspect of religious law, is pre-eminent even in the cases of historically unique personalities. All the important Jewish figures and tendencies are so comprehended that, even in the story of Abraham, for example, the problems of *Halakhah* supervene. Thus it is natural that for the Talmud the conflicts between the Pharisees and their adversaries had a pre-eminently *Halakhah* character.

To understand what actually separated the Pharisees from the rest of the people, two factors must be kept in mind. In the first place, the one thing that most sharply distinguished the Pharisees from their adversaries, the Sadducees, is something that Josephus reported quite incidentally and without particularly trying to accommodate himself to the ideas of his Greek and Roman readers. In relating how the opposition manifested itself for the first time in the political sphere, in a struggle for power, he says: "The Pharisees, on the basis of tradition, teach the people many precepts that are not recorded in the law of Moses. For that very reason the party of the Sadducees rejects them, declaring that it is commanded that the written precepts be observed, but that the precepts taught on the basis of the teachings of the fathers be not observed." [15]

Accordingly, Josephus tells us in the same passage that John Hyrcanus, when he turned away from the Pharisees and joined the Sadducees, "abolished the precepts they had introduced among the people and punished those who observed them." [16] Thus the opposition between the Pharisees and Sadducees, or, in the words of Josephus, "that concerning which they had great disputes and differences," is here explicitly related to the question of the validity of the traditional precepts not contained in the Scriptures—the validity of what Hebrew sources refer to as the "words of the Soferim," or the "words of the sages."

Concerning those who taught these precepts, Josephus again, in a casual, non-tendentious passage, makes a definite statement. He says that they "had a high regard for the exact study of the law inherited from the fathers," [17] that they "interpreted the laws more accurately," [18] that they "were regarded as men distinguished from all others by the accuracy of their teachings of the law of the fathers," [19] and "as those who expounded the precepts with exactitude." [20] In the Acts of the Apostles (22:3), Paul similarly boasts of being "a man . . . brought up in this city at the feet of Gamaliel, and taught according to the perfect manner of the law of the fathers." Characteristically, in all these passages the same Greek word, *akribeia*, which means "accurate" or "perfect of its kind," is used in its various forms. It is intended to express approximately the same concept as the Hebrew *Darash* and *Midrash*, respectively *Lamad* and *Talmud*, in the meaning they had at that time. The men who taught these precepts were in fact the men of this "accuracy" or "perfection," of this *akribeia* or *Midrash;* they sought to give the words, and above all the law of the Bible, their full and accurate meaning. They were the vehicles of the "Oral Torah," which was now added to the "Written Torah"; they interpreted it and continued it. The search for the exact meaning and the ultimate law to which they were committed was for them an ever-renewed revelation of the Book, a perpetual comparing of the Book with reality.

Our term *Darash*, and expressions that correspond almost exactly to those used by Josephus, occur with reference to Ezra, who is praised for having conceived it as his task "to seek the law of the Lord, and to do it and to teach in Israel statutes

14

and the ordinances" (Ezra 7:10). And it is no accident that he should have been the first of whom this was said. With him there began in Palestine a development that had been prepared and carried through in Babylonia. Since the Babylonian Exile, in addition to the sacrificial service, which retained its historical significance, there had appeared, first in Babylonia and then in Palestine, the new divine service, consisting of prayer, the reading of passages from the Scriptures, and, as a necessary corollary, the explanation of the Scriptures. The synagogue with its divine service took a place beside the Temple, the seat of the sacrifice. Even before the destruction of the Second Temple, this service was considered as something so customary and essential in the life of the nation that its basic elements were considered to go back to the very beginnings of the religion of Israel. The numerous houses in which this new form of worship was practised could be found not only in the eastern and western Diasporas, but also and above all in Palestine, the land of the Temple, near that old center of worship. The author of Psalm 74, which probably dates from the period of the Maccabean struggle, mentions the "sanctuary," "the dwelling-place of Thy name," and "the meeting-places of God in the land," one beside the other, as belonging together.

This juxtaposition of the Temple and synagogue was possible when harmony prevailed, particularly since the Temple had incorporated into its worship an essential element of the new ritual, prayer. But sooner or later the two were bound to come into conflict. Inevitably the question had to be raised as to which was the actual religious hearth of the nation, that is, which was the real seat of the divine service, the Temple or the synagogues. And it is understandable, considering the crucial importance ascribed to the Bible, that all the parties in this controversy attempted to base their claims upon it. The tannaitic tradition shows this clearly. Here the question of what is the real divine service, the *Avodah*, is often discussed. And the answer given is that the "service of God" is not the sacrifice that took place in the Temple but the prayer and the explanation of the Scriptures that took place in the synagogue.

Especially the explanation of the Scriptures—what Josephus emphasized—was stressed. All the passages that put forward this point of view—anonymous Haggadah—obviously date from the period when the Temple was still opposed to the synagogues. We know many relevant passages dating from the generations after its destruction, especially by Yohanan ben Zakkai and his disciples. They express a conciliatory desire; they point out that the seat of the sacrificial service had not become empty, that what it had bestowed in the past was not lost, that now prayer, good deeds and repentance had taken its place. A comparison of the earlier with the later passages clearly shows the difference in attitude. The latter were intended as consolation in the face of what has already happened, in the face of destiny; the former unmistakably express the struggle to discover a higher principle in the face of something that exists.

Above all, it is preoccupation with the teachings, as we have said, that is presented as the higher, true divine service. The words of the section of Deuteronomy (11:3) that became the second part of the *Shema* prayer and also were part of the morning devotions of the priests in the Temple, "Thou shalt love the Lord, thy God, and serve Him with all thy heart and all thy soul" are commented upon in the Sifre as follows: " 'To serve Him'—that means study of the Torah . . . just as service of the altar is called divine service, so is the study of the Torah." [21] And the additional explanation is given that this is "the first commandment of God, which was given the first man, before all sacrificial service and all service in the sanctuary." [22]

Likewise, in another text, divine service through the Torah is placed above divine service in the Temple: " 'Thou shalt serve the Lord' means: Serve him through his Torah and in his sanctuary." [23] Even more explicit is a text transmitted by the school of Rabbi Akiba in the Sifre on Numbers. The precept that the Levites should keep the charge of the tabernacle whatsoever the service of the tabernacle may be (Num. 18:4), is here explained as follows: " 'Charge of the tabernacle' means the dogmas and all service; all *Avodah* in the tabernacle means study of the Torah." [24] The antagonism to the sacrificial service cannot be mistaken here. In this connection, there is a characteristic text that probably dates only from the period following the destruction of the Temple and that is contained in both *Mekhiltot*. It enumerates everything for which Israel became a martyr and which for that reason is its permanent possession, and then everything for which Israel did not become a martyr, and which for that reason is not its permanent possession. And among the first, study of the Torah is mentioned, whereas among the latter, we find the Temple. Here, too, it is clear that the Temple, as the seat of the divine service, has at last receded into the background.

In a similar way, prayer, the second element of the divine service in the synagogue, is opposed to the sacrificial service. The words from Deuteronomy quoted above, "Thou shalt love the Lord, thy God, and serve Him with all thy heart and all thy soul," are also commented upon as follows: " 'To serve Him,' that means prayer; for when it is said: 'To serve with all thy heart,' what else can this service with the heart be but prayer. As service at the altar is named service of God, *Avodah,* so prayer is named service of God." [25] Accordingly, in the Palestinian Targum, the words "Him shall ye serve" (Deut. 13:5) are translated as "ye shall pray unto Him." [26] This coincides with the explanation of the words "Ye shall serve the Lord your God" (Exod. 23:25) that is found in the Talmud and that runs as follows: "This means the reading of the *Shema* and the *Tefillah,* the Prayer of Benedictions." [27] Another tradition, which the Palestinian Talmud attributes to Rabbi Menahem of Gallaya, probably also dates from early times, and runs as follows: "To him who comes before the shrine of the Torah in order to recite the *Tefillah,* one shall not say: come and pray, but step you forward: perform our sacrifice, do what we need, wage our struggle, implore atonement for us." [28] Here, too, in all these sentences, we can recognize that another mode of worship, prayer, is being installed not only side by side with the sacrifice but in opposition to it; and that in justification for this the weighty evidence of the Scriptures is adduced.

There is other evidence pointing in the same direction. Thus, we find in the Mishnah a number of precepts which, to say the least, do not seem friendly towards the special rights of the priesthood, and in which many privileges previously granted to the priests are here granted to the people. Furthermore, there are hard words, dating from the tannaitic period, directed against the aristocratic priestly families and their special claims; and with regard to the priestly blessing, it is stated emphatically that "the blessing does not depend upon the priests," that "the priests have not the right to say: we bless Israel." [29] And contrary evidence cannot be found in the fact that some prominent Pharisees, at the time of the Temple, belonged to the priestly class, as for instance, Jose ben Yoezer, "the devout one among the priests," Hananiah, who was probably the last "chief of the priests," and perhaps also Yohanan ben Zakkai. Despite the conflict between the Pharisees and the priests, some Pharisees were priests, just as in Rome, in the struggle between patricians and plebeians, there were patricians who were at the same time the victorious leaders of the plebeians.

A further indication of the role of the Pharisees and their significance to the people is apparent in the following: the Pharisees, with clear and imperative decisiveness, introduced over and above the Temple service exclusively performed by the priests, a mode of divine service that the whole people could perform independently in its synagogue by means of prayer and study of the Bible. In this sense they can be called the people's party, which fought against the privileged position and hereditary prerogatives of the priests. Thus their most determined adversaries were the priestly aristocracy of the Sadducees.

The priestly position was undermined in another respect, almost to a greater extent than the synagogical claims had impugned its ancient privilege of conducting divine service: the men of the synagogue laid claim to, and then gradually won, the right to administer the law. In Deuteronomy, the administration of justice was acknowledged as pre-eminently the priest's, just as Leviticus, "the priestly law," entrusts him with deciding what is clean and unclean. At the time of the Exile and immediately after it the priest was also entrusted with the Torah, "the Torah is sought from his mouth." [30] Even in the Book of Ezra we see the priest teaching the Torah and summoning the people to abide by it. But there is something else apparent in Ezra, a new factor introduced in the course of the Babylonian Exile. During the Exile, the priests were barred from performing their first and essential office—the sacrificial service; what they retained of their old rights was only the custody and administration of the Torah.

Thus we are confronted with a new phenomenon: men whose particular task and highest mission are to study and to teach the Torah. The first historical figure in whom this is realized is Ezra. He was a priest, and is so mentioned, but his real role is the *Sofer*, the *grammateus*, the man of the Book. This term, which had previously denoted the learned official, now acquired a new meaning: "scribe in the Law of Moses" (Ezra 7:6), "scribe of the words of the commandments of the Lord and of his statutes to Israel" (Ezra 7:11). How quickly this came to be accepted can be seen from the fact that in the Book of Sirach it is already taken for granted; here the Sofer and his talent, the quality of *misparut* or *grammateia*, are universally referred to. In the First and Second Maccabees mention is already made of the "scribes." In the Book of Sirach we also find the expression *Bet ha-Midrash*, "house of study," and *Yeshivah*, "circle of the students"; thus all these conceptions were present even in pre-Maccabean times.

On Palestinian ground these concepts must have acquired meanings different from those they had had in Babylonia. For the Temple was reconstructed after the captivity, and the sacrificial service was reintroduced. Thus the priests won back their original function and privileges. It was only natural that the function they had recovered should have caused their other function, the exposition of the Torah, to retreat into the background; it was probably the case that the priests thus often lacked a thorough knowledge of the Torah. It was also natural that the province increasingly forsaken by many of the priests should be taken over by others, non-priests, who explicitly claimed it as their own. Thus the term "scribe" began to denote not only the priest, but another class that occupied a position either adjoining the priestly one or opposed to it.

This development can be clearly followed. While in the Book of Sirach it still could be said that God had entrusted his commandments to the priesthood "and had given them the administration of the precepts and the law, that they might teach the precepts to their people and the law to the children of Israel" (45:17), the Second Maccabees already says that "God restored the heritage to all, and the kingdom and the priesthood and the hallowing" (2:17). And the same idea is expressed in similar, and even more emphatic terms, in the tannaitic tradition, which explains the biblical phrase, "the portion and the inheritance" (Num. 18:20) of the priesthood, as follows: "There are three crowns: the crown of the Torah, the crown of the priesthood, the crown of the kingdom . . . The crown of the Torah is offered to everyone, and he who has won it stands before God as though all three had been offered him, and he had won them all." [31]

Thus the administration of justice, which at first had been the privilege of the priests, now became the privilege of all the people. Not because he is a priest but only when he is a scribe is the priest recognized as a judge. The scribe supplants the priest so that in the end the Tannaim, by virtue of their role as interpreters of the law, almost abolish the priests' old biblical function; they declare that a tribunal is legitimate even without priests and Levites. The assertion made in the introductory sentence of the Sayings of the Fathers, according to which the line of scribes are the successors and heirs of the High Priest Simeon the Just, although unhistorical, is entirely justified and in the tradition of the Torah. This evolution finds its completion, so to speak, in the words of Deuteronomy about the obedience owed the priests who sit in judgment: "Thou shalt not turn aside from the sentence which they shall declare unto thee, to the right hand, nor to the left" (Deut. 17:11). They were understood as a command to recognize everything ordained by the scribes.

The ultimate conclusion to be drawn from the literature of the period of the Second Temple is that the Pharisaic trend found its leaders in the scribes. This does not mean that only the Pharisees had scribes, or that all the scribes were Pharisees. There is no doubt that the period of the conflict between the Pharisees and the Sadducees was also a period of intellectual controversy, and that the Sadducees too, at least at that time, had their scribes. Moreover, the pursuit of their judicial activities demanded a knowledge of biblical law and the ability to interpret it. Scriptural erudition must have nevertheless been of more importance to and more characteristic of the Pharisees. In their case, only their knowledge and their teaching could have given them the authority, position, and importance that had always been the priest's by virtue of his origin and office. The praise that Josephus, at the end of his *Jewish Antiquities*, accords his people, and that he also intends as a characterization of the scribes, is particularly applicable to the Pharisees: "They attribute wisdom only to those who have a clear knowledge of the precepts and are able to explain the whole meaning of the Scriptures." [32]

Moreover, the Pharisees, to a greater extent than the others, were prominent figures, especially in the spiritual life. If hardly any names of Sadducean scribes have come down to us, this cannot be due only to the fact that the tradition of the whole period ultimately remained in the hands of the Pharisaic scholars. True, they alone, so far as we know, established the genealogical tree of the tradition; they did this, if for no other purpose, to prove the legitimacy of their teachings by virtue of the uninterrupted succession of their teachers. The few scribes mentioned by Josephus, however, are men who we know were Pharisees; he, too, fails to mention any Sadducean scribes. The reason that only Pharisaic scribes are known to us may thus lie in the circumstance that scriptural erudition, which necessarily evolved from Pharisaism, was essentially its province. Although not exclusively the possession of the Pharisees, it was a characteristic feature of their movement.

In all the ancient written testimonies the Pharisaic tendency thus appears as a distinct and determining path in the evolution of the Jewish people. Its beginning, which definitely pointed the way to its future development, belongs to the Babylonian Exile; there it started out; it derived its character, its reason, and its meaning from it. In Jewish history this exile was the first great selection, a decisive winnowing that resulted in the survival of only the "most useful." The few became many, because only the few strong ones could survive. In the eyes of the majority, the fall of the state and the destruction of the Temple emphatically proved that the gods of the victors were victorious. Later, surrounded by the wonders of the Babylonian world, they must have again imagined themselves overcome; it must have seemed to them that the life and people of this new world were superior to themselves and their old pious modes of existence. The ruins on Zion and the palaces on the Euphrates exercised an equal effect. Both spoke the same language, and for many there was only one inference to be drawn: the Jews must capitulate inwardly as well as outwardly to Babylonia and the heathen gods.

Those who thought thus and acted accordingly sooner or later ceased to be Jews. But the rest, these few out of many, because they were determined to remain faithful, were now grown able to resist the effects of time; they had something of the prophets' intransigent strength. Only those possessed that strength who were certain of the unique character of their religion and their chosenness, and this very certainty gave them an inflexible determination to survive and an abiding hope in their future. The great necessity of choosing between Israel and Babylonia formed the men whose grandsons were able to follow Ezra along the way that was not the way of the others, whose descendants were able to wage the battles of the Maccabees and the protracted struggle against Rome. Men of their mold were also the ancestors of the Zealots and the Essenes. This was the time in which history made its selection.

The effect of history is to lead those who withstand such a process of selection—thus becoming aware of themselves—to a point of separation. What necessity requires, is willed: the realization of one's difference is transformed into a resolution to be different. That was what took place in the Babylonian Exile. When these men realized that they, and in all likelihood the generations after them, would have to live in Babylonia, they were forced, in the interests of their spiritual self-preservation, to attempt the creation of a world in which they could lead their own lives. This world, this community, had to be created amidst all the seductions the Babylonian civilization offered. Only within a circle of people separated from the others could they remain inwardly secure and preserve in themselves the character they had to have in order to inhabit the realm of Babylonia and the inner realm of Judaism at the same time, in order to fulfil the solemn promise of Jeremiah, the prophet, to the exiles, and at the same time lead their separate "community" life: "And seek the peace of the city whither I have caused you to be carried away captive, and pray unto the Lord for it: for in the peace thereof shall ye have peace" (Jer. 29:7).

This decision defined what ought to be the goal of every impulse towards self-realization, and the paths leading to it. All hope depended upon circumscribing and thereby preserving the world of Judaism, upon the resolve, for its sake, to live in the midst of the new world one might almost say as on an island. Separateness and isolation had to be erected into a principle. This could be done with all the more energy since all thinking and acting, in so far as it did not serve only the individual, now had a clear goal. Everything that in Palestine had attracted and absorbed men's energies, all desire for position, all political and party interests, were absent here. The will that heretofore had so often been turned outward, now, in so far as it transcended purely personal considerations, was directed inward. So long as it sought to pass beyond the limits of the present moment and its cares, it could find the true home of its spirit in the genius of its religion. The will to inner strength took the place of all aspirations to power.

Here for the first time in history a religious congregation was formed; here was a community lacking an ancestral ground, lacking the support of a state, separated from what constituted elsewhere, and heretofore for itself as well, the natural conditions of community life; a community placed in the midst of a different and wondrous world, and yet filled with the living certainty of the need to remain independent. Here, for the first time, people outside their own country constituted themselves a community in the name of religion. True, racial consciousness with its many memories survived and proved itself a strong bond; true, also, that the hopes for a rebirth of the nation and a restoration of the state united all the ideas of the future into the idea of the collectivity. But among those who survived the catastrophe and mastered it inwardly, the factor that directly held their present existence together—the consciousness of being different and belonging together in and through their religion—played a far more effective role than the traditions of the past and the promise of the future. Even in the prophetic speeches of that time, which express these memories and hopes, this more immediate consideration can be recognized.

A congregation of faith arose, and within it many smaller congregations; the same words—*Edah, Kahal, Keneset, Tzibbur*—denoted the congregation as a whole and the individual congregations comprised in it. It supplied what until then and everywhere else was supplied only by political bonds. Equally with the separation brought about by selection, the united community of Judaism constituted the principle, motive, and goal of Pharisaism. The movement begins in the community, and always strives to return to it.

The universalism heralded by the prophets, above all by the second great prophet of the Exile, the so-called Deutero-Isaiah, was not impaired by this development. On the contrary, it had prepared the firm ground that served as a vantage point for the wide-ranging view of universalism. It was precisely the congregation and its congregations that provided Judaism a missionary starting point, and it was this that attracted the proselytes. The "isolated" congregation became an evangelical one.

The concept and consciousness of universalism achieved a particular expression in it, moreover, because the idea of *Hokhmah*, wisdom, here received its form and meaning, its Midrash. It is an old biblical idea, and already in the Bible it denoted not only the knowledge of and desire for the good and the just, this true fear of God, but also (in the eighth chapter of Proverbs) a world-creating force, the Reason by virtue of which the cosmos came into being. It was this very meaning that now took hold of men's minds. Moreover, it also gave the Bible a new meaning. For the Bible, the Torah, was now often identified with *Hokhmah*. Already for Joshua ben Sirach this was an important idea, and since his time it has remained a frequent Midrash: the Torah is the *Hokhmah*, the *Hokhmah* is the Torah.

Thus the Book became something more than a book—it became a cosmic force in which all creativeness and form originated. It became what in the later Judeo-Alexandrian writings is the *logos*, God's creative thought, existent since time eternal. The community of this book was also raised to another world— it became something that had existed since the beginning of things. Just as the vastness of the cosmos, the universalism of infinity, permeated the thinking of the "separated," so, in a sense, it permeated the congregation. The congregation has its place on earth, but it also has an ideal, almost mystical, extension in the cosmos. It belonged to the cosmos as much as and almost more than to the earth.

Eschatological Messianism, a specific feature of Pharisaism, also derives from this element. The doctrine of the Messiah and of the "days to come" was an old heritage dating from the prophets; it had always been the "comfort of Israel," as it was now piously expressed. But at this period it also acquired new features. Already in the Book of Daniel it was apparent how, to the contrast between "now" and "some day," which determined the prophetic idea of the Messiah, had been added the contrast between "here below" and "above," between "this world" and "the hereafter." Men's thought now began to be preoccupied with two concepts: "this world," and "the world to come." The Messiah belongs to this "world to come," the true world; when he appears, the "world to come" will have been realized here below, and this world and the hereafter will become one. The Messiah, just like the *Hokhmah*, the Torah, the *logos*, or the congregation, becomes a cosmic entity, a cosmic principle, dwelling in God from the beginning of time, ready to descend on the day of fulfilment.

As a result, the doctrine of the Messiah was increasingly endowed with eschatological features; it became what was an often curious doctrine of the final days of the world. That ultimate question, full of hope and anxiety, of the last day, laid hold of people's minds. Thus a cosmic element was introduced into the congregation's yearning to participate directly in the experience of the final moment. The notion of resurrection shaped its imagination, but the essential element in it remained the intense thoughts of the world to come, which expressed a deep spiritual need. The basic idea of Pharisaism demanded justification by the beyond. Isolation could not find its meaning in itself; it could only be the path commanded of the Jews to an ultimate human fulfilment, to a universal goal, a path, as it were, from this world to the next. A deep longing for the ultimate—Josephus bears unmistakable witness to this —must have at all times filled the Pharisees, and it endowed both their isolation and their interpretation of the Scriptures with a tendency towards the infinite and universal.

However, in addition to this cosmic element, a human element was introduced in an unexpected way, and this again in the doctrine of the *Hokhmah*. For the original meaning of the *Hokhmah* was this, too: a wisdom that is the share not only of the people to whom the revelation had been given but also of "the nations." In the biblical books dealing with it—Proverbs, Job, Ecclesiastes—this wisdom does not speak to the Jews alone, it speaks to man. The idea of its identity with the Torah is therefore always accompanied by the idea that it is the share of man, even though in Job the last answer is the revealed one, and thus reserved to God. Here the term "man" acquires its right accent. It is significant that among the Pharisees some believed that Job, the man who was "whole-hearted and upright, and one that feared God and shunned evil," (Job 1:1) Job, the protagonist of the drama between God and His accuser, Satan, was a non-Jew.

The Bible contains many passages pointing in this direction; thus Balaam, the Aramaean, is the man to whom God reveals himself, and Cyrus, the king of Persia, is the "shepherd" of the Lord, his "anointed." But the decisive impulse towards universalism was given by the ethical conception of the *Hokhmah*, developed in conjunction with the cosmic one: wisdom as the wisdom of man. Thus it could be said in grateful benediction on a non-Jew: "Blessed art thou, O Lord, who hast given man of thy wisdom." Such was the teaching of the men of the "isolation." Here, too, they prepared the way for the message of Judaism. Judeo-Hellenistic humanism also had its beginnings in the concept of *Hokhmah*. Thus, thanks to its very differences, the Jewish community in isolation could preserve its connection with humanity.

In the middle of this far-flung world of the spirit the congregation also had a visible symbol. It had very early set up a recognizable place and center in its houses of worship, which expressed both its solidarity with and its separateness from the others. The home of worship shaped the congregation. By its means the Jews were able to achieve an inner and spiritual mastery over the fact of the fall of the Temple and, as is the case with all spiritual conquests, they thus were able to realize a higher principle. They prepared the way for the non-sacrificial divine service; they erected their new house of worship as a "house of prayer"—we hear this term for the first time from the great prophet of the second generation of the Exile. The many synagogues took the place of the one Temple. A new form of the house of worship, which later imposed itself upon the world, was thus created. To what extent community and house were identified is seen from the fact that on the one hand the house of worship was referred to as *Bet ha-Keneset,* "the house of assembly" (of the community), and that on the other hand the same term "synagogue" once denoted both the community and its house of worship.

Only this made it possible for the congregation to be divided into congregations. Within the great whole smaller areas with their local centers were formed, and thus the whole was organically articulated. Thus it was possible to integrate every individual more fully, for he belonged to a local religious community and was forever vitally connected with its particular locality. While the Temple was the possession only of the people as a whole, and only indirectly, the synagogue belonged to each of them directly.· As against the aristocratic Temple, the synagogue had a democratic character. The intensification of spiritual life that had been the result of the sifting of the Jewish nation was thus preserved, and it remained a permanent trait. It alone made the Pharisaic movement possible. Its point of departure and its support was the synagogue, and it perpetually drew its strength from it.

At the same time the house of the new divine service was allotted a special day of the week. The Sabbath, that "sign between God and the children of Israel," acquired a new meaning. It became the day of the divine service, and the synagogue could also be referred to as the "house of the Sabbath." And the Sabbath thus became the day of the Book, just as the synagogue became the "house of the Book." The Scriptures were recited in the house of worship on every Sabbath, and thereby a form was created that later was adopted and developed by other nations. The Holy Scriptures now became the Scriptures of the people, the possession of each individual. This, too, was a democratic step. As the book of the divine service, the Bible was no longer the exclusive possession of the priests, nor yet a mere book. As the prayer service, so the service of the Book was entrusted to all; in this, too, every man was a priest. The Torah, formerly the Torah of the priests, was now the Torah of the people. It became, in the words of the Greek translation of the blessing of Moses, "the heritage of the congregations, of the synagogues of Jacob." The synagogues and their Book actually abolished the special privilege of the priesthood.

The price paid for this was nevertheless a high one. For if the Book became the book of the people, and thus the people became the People of the Book, not only the priesthood, but also the prophets who had created this Book and put the innermost strivings of their soul into it lost to a great extent their place and their former significance. In a fundamental sense they now became superfluous. Religious truth derived from this book, which was the purest source of the Jewish teachings. And if this was so, the prophecy was bound to recede into the background and ultimately disappear. It is noteworthy that the term *Darash*, which in the Bible signified the interrogation of and search for God, now became the proper term for the interrogation and study of the Scriptures. The religious personality no longer found, or at least did not only find, its sanction in itself and its religious force, but in its relation to the Book. This fact is clearly expressed in the following passage from the Palestinian Talmud: "The prophet and the scribe are messengers of God; the prophet needs the seal of God, the sign and the miracle, the scribe does not need it, for he proves himself by the Torah." [33] This sentence correctly describes the course and results of the development we have described above. The prophet was supplanted by the scribe. The authority of the Scriptures gave him who taught them his special authority. It is for this reason that in the Gospels the authenticity of its Messiah is not only attested to by the miracles he is said to have performed but above all by the word of the Book. "According to the Scriptures," "that this that is written might be fulfilled," is always put forward as the final proof.

This development began at a very early time, as early as the beginning of the Exile. Isaiah learned of his mission when he felt the burning coal upon his lips, and by hearing the voice of the Lord, saying: "Whom shall I send, and who will go for us?" (Isa. 6:8). Jeremiah acquired his conviction in a similar way: "Then the Lord put forth His hand and touched my mouth. And the Lord said unto me: Behold, I have put My words in thy mouth. See, I have this day set thee over the nations and over the kingdoms" (Jer. 1:9-10). But later Ezekiel was given his mission by the waters of Babylon in the following manner: "And when I looked, behold, a hand was put forth unto me; and, lo, a roll of a book was therein . . . And He said unto me: 'Son of man, eat what thou findest; eat this roll, and go, speak unto the House of Israel'" (Ezek. 2:9; 3:1). These different ways in which God reveals himself are not merely differences in metaphor—they are differences arising from a process of development. The hand that touched Isaiah's lips and put the words into Jeremiah's mouth gave Ezekiel the book. Here the man of the word heralds the man of the book, the prophet heralds the Sofer, the Scribe. Ezekiel is still predominantly a prophet; but in Ezra—although he, too, doubtless had prophetic features (the Targum ascribes the prophetic speeches of Malachi to him)—the lineaments of the man of the Scriptures are pronounced.

This does not mean that the unfettered religious impulse was checked, much less entirely stopped, by this development; it continued to operate, although in a different manner. For the place of the prophet was taken not only by the scribe but also by the psalmist and the poet of prayer. And above all a strong religious certainty, something of the spirit that had lived in the prophet, now came alive both in the congregation and the individual. The very fact that the congregation was built upon the individual and the individual's personal achievement represented a different and unique feature. While the Temple was a place chosen and given by God, and was not conceived of as something created by man, the synagogue was in a very real sense the work of man; it depended upon his personal will and personal action. While the old worship was a matter for the people as a whole, the new divine service was a matter for each individual. Through the synagogues the individual acquired his place.

The value of the individual was now extraordinarily enhanced by this opportunity to make the Torah his own. Each man could know it "in his mouth and in his heart," so that he could speak in the name of God's Book, and hence, as it were, in the name of God Himself. The words "It [the commandment] is not in heaven" (Deut. 30:12) now acquired their full pathos. Now man could oppose himself and his knowledge of the truth even to what presented itself to him as a miracle. Now his judgment could have greater validity than a *Bat Kol*, a heavenly voice. The word of God is in the Book, and it asserts its rights against everything.[34] The "here I stand, I cannot do otherwise" derived its strongest expression from this; and martyrdom, which was so widespread throughout the whole period, found one of its roots here. Faith in the words of the testimony helped to create the martyr, or witness of the faith.

There was still another element in this development from which the individual drew religious strength. He was given the Book, the whole Book, and thus he was also entrusted with the whole commandment. The constant imperative of the Bible, its great and constant "thou shalt," was addressed to every man; the totality of religious duty was now his. At that time the law became the Jew's life possession. The Bible's solemn summons to the will, the compelling knowledge that man is created by God and is in the hand of God, that he is called to choose the path of duty and fulfilment—this earnestness towards life now became a predominant feature of the Jewish congregation. What Josephus says of the Pharisees— that they believed in the divine dispensation, but also in the freedom of human choice—and what Rabbi Akiba later expressed in the sentence: "Everything is determined, but freedom is given," [35] is neither more nor less than the great paradox by which the Bible lives, the paradox that the living creature, God's handiwork, is nevertheless confronted with the eternally-demanding but never-fulfilled commandment. That is how the Book is to be understood according to the teaching of the Pharisees. Only if all this is taken into consideration can the presuppositions and distinctive features of Pharisaism be understood.

In addition to Pharisaism, another factor contributed to endowing the word of the Book with a sacred character. At that time Aramaic became the everyday language in Babylonia and Palestine; thus Hebrew, the language of the Bible, could become "the language of the holy." [36] This factor, too, contributed to making the Bible the "Holy Scriptures." The remoteness of sacred things, the holiness inherent in them, now characterized the Bible, which was thus raised above everything profane. And those who possessed the Bible acquired something of this. The distinctiveness of their language seemed to make them in some degree different, separate, almost sacred. In addition to the language that joined them to those around them, they had a language that kept them separated. This, too, contributed to their becoming a "congregation."

A new task arose as a result. If the Bible was to be the Book of all the people, it had to be translated into the language of the people. All translation is commentary, and it was especially so in this instance, because the content of the Bible was usually far removed from daily life. The Scriptures began to need the scribe. In the translation, the Targum, the Midrash, is already prefigured; there is already in it the beginnings of both the *Halakhah* and the Haggadah. Thus there was created the task

35

of constantly renewing the Bible and the means to accomplish this task. The Targum and Midrash prevented the Bible from petrifying in its sacredness. The Bible had to be put into the language of people, and for that reason it had to be grasped inwardly ever anew, and conquered ever anew. Its teachings could never be something consummated or complete. A first requirement of the "Oral Law" was already expressed in the fact that the language of the Bible differed from everyday language. This was the beginning of that *akribeia,* "accuracy" or "perfection," which later became an attribute of Pharisaism.

Separation from its native ground and the new tasks and conditions of existence with which the Exile confronted it made Judaism undergo a new formative process. All the distinctive features of Pharisaism were prefigured in this new process and determined by it. But, as we have shown above, it achieved its historical form only in Palestine. In Babylonia the new tendencies, so far as we have been able to discover, asserted themselves without engendering any basic conflict, and were determined wholly by the internal logic of the situation. For that reason the process in Babylonia soon came to a halt, and it was lacking for a long time in any men of note. It likewise was lacking in the Haggadah, that living witness to the existence of spiritual struggle. But in Palestine the conflict and the controversies were soon in full swing. The ancestral land served over and over again as a battlefield for the contest of minds, as well as for those contests in which blood was shed. Pharisaism was formed and developed in this recurrent conflict, which often passed over into war. Pharisaism was able in this conflict to realize the effective vigor of its principles and the consistency and intransigence of its thinking; here it acquired its variety of ideas and its wealth of figures. Pharisaism proper belongs to Palestine and Palestine's particular history.

The importance of the homeland lay indeed less in the conflicts it engendered than in the continuation of that process of selection by which only the resolute and the firm survived. This selection was a recurrent process. When those who returned from exile erected their dwellings, they found themselves surrounded by "the peoples of the lands" and were forced to remain in contact with them. Since any steps taken towards them were bound to lead to a mingling with them, the former exiles, for the sake of their separateness, had to oppose them, rejecting any and all alliances, and dissolving whatever alliances had already been made. This first sifting of the people in the new Palestine was the work of two strong personalities, Ezra and Nehemiah, who conceived it as their mission to bring the spirit of the congregation to Palestine and insure its triumph there. It was then that the Jews of the land became *Nivdalim*, or separated ones. The other sifting process took place in a later epoch when, as a result of Alexander's victories, Asia Minor and Egypt, between which lay Palestine, became a part of the Hellenistic world. Until that time the face of Palestine had been turned to the East; now it turned to the Mediterranean. Hellenism at first attracted the attention of the people, and finally the people themselves. It was in the Maccabean war, above all in its spiritual and intellectual battles, that the Jews waged their great and decisive struggle for the preservation of their genius against this new world. The Maccabean war, too, produced men separated from the others, men who were able and determined to defend and develop their own world.

Both externally and internally, this era had the most far-reaching consequences; it was at this time that the real Pharisaism first appeared on the historical scene. The sifting process continued throughout the period during which the degenerate descendants of the Maccabeans created internal dissension in the country and Rome intervened in the history of Judea, her puppets and later her officials becoming the rulers of the land. The struggle for an individual existence became a continuous one; steadfast effort was needed to carry it on. This need produced two movements alongside the main trend of Pharisaism. One was that of the Zealots, who wanted to wage the struggle with the sword, as the Maccabeans had done once before. The Zealots were their heirs in intention, if not in results. The other was that of the Essenes, who chose to survive the struggle by yielding the tyrant his domain and dwelling on the far-off plains at the edge of the country. This tendency was strengthened by a temper of mind that went back to the prophet Elijah, and by traditions and ideas stemming from the ancient Rehabites, who did not "build house, nor sow seed, nor plant vineyard," but dwelled all their days in tents (Jer. 35:7). Such feelings had probably never quite disappeared among the people—moods of exasperation with the city and urban forms of existence, a yearning for direct contact with nature and for the free tents that were the dwellings of the fathers when they followed God in the desert, in the days of the revelation. Surely there was no lack of controversies in the course of which the extreme personalities in each camp reproached the moderates for not taking the ideal seriously enough. But all of them belonged to the same Pharisaic movement; by exacting "separateness," they all sought to make secure a uniquely Jewish domain. The sifting process and the will to it, the will to be separate, were the determining factors in both these movements.

In addition to this sifting process, as we have said, there was the conflict of the Jews amongst themselves. It was first of all a conflict with the priests, with their privileges and traditions, the conflict between synagogue and Temple. In Babylonia this split could not manifest itself, for there nothing within the community competed with the synagogue. There the priests were private individuals, not a class with an official position. But here, in Palestine, side by side with the synagogues and above them, was the new Temple built by those returned from exile, and its priests were pre-eminent among the people. In the days when the new Palestinian community was established, the priests were its architects and assistants; later, when there was the battle to be waged against Greek influence and foreign usurpation, they were pioneers and heroes. Joshua ben Jehozadak, the leader of the homecomers, Zechariah, their prophet, and then Ezra, the creator of the new community, were all of the family of priests, as were the Maccabees who won the new free state by force of arms. The priests enjoyed an acknowledged position on the soil of Palestine, not only by virtue of their office and hereditary rights, but also by virtue of their historic achievements.

Thus the conflict was an irrepressible one. The two forms of the divine service could not simply remain juxtaposed. An ingenious attempt was indeed made to establish a fundamental connection between them and to establish the populace as co-adjutor to the priests in the divine service. Already, early during the period of the Second Temple, the institution of the so-called *Maamadot,* or popular representatives, arose. The districts of the Holy Land, one each week, sent deputations to

39

Jerusalem, who represented the people at the sacrificial service, thus clearly giving it the character of a collective service. And four times a day these deputations, as well as those who remained at home, held divine services consisting of prayers and recitation of the Scriptures. But little by little—as though impelled by an inner logic—one type of divine service sought to predominate over and repel the influence of the other. Although the Pharisees acknowledged the Temple—it was, after all, prescribed in the Book and indissolubly joined with biblical history—and although they fought beside the priests in its defense, the antagonism could never be entirely eliminated. Both the Temple and the synagogues had an established position in the land and demanded general recognition: the constant recrudescence of the antagonism was inevitable. The Pharisees, in their role of the men of the synagogue, stood opposed to the Sadducees, the men of the Temple.

The Sadducees had a strong ally. The Temple and its sacrifices are mentioned in the Bible, especially in its most canonical book, the Torah; prayer is not mentioned in it at all. Thus the synagogue prayer was not "biblical," only the sacrifice was. The priests could appeal to the scriptural text. It is probably this that gave a big impulse to the Pharisaic need to go beyond the word and explain and interpret the Bible. The divine service of the synagogue had first to justify itself through the Midrash, the "Oral Law"; it had to demonstrate by means of the Midrash, as we have seen, that prayer and scriptural recital were in truth the *Avodah,* the divine service. This is a further instance of the association of the synagogue with oral law. But it is also understandable how the conflict thus grew more acute. The opposition between the two types of divine service had to extend to the manner of understanding the Bible and to the whole basis of the religion.

Moreover, if separateness was something that was commanded to all the people—and this was the way the Pharisees understood it—there was no longer any room for a separate class of priests. This Pharisaic idea had a classical precedent in Judaism. At bottom, it expresses only what is expressed in the old commandment that introduces the revelation on Mount Sinai: "Ye shall be unto Me a kingdom of priests, and a holy nation" (Exod. 19:6), or as the Targum translates it: "Ye shall be unto my Name kings, priests, and a holy nation." Priestly privilege in any form was incompatible with the idea of the priesthood of all, an idea to which the Pharisees now attempted to give its full meaning. The Second Maccabees, a book that celebrates the liberation of the Temple and the deeds of the men of the family of priests, and that is already informed by the awakening Pharisaic spirit, expresses the idea of this biblical phrase even more clearly in the solemn message that closes the introductory chapters: "Now God who saved all his people, and restored the heritage to all, and the kingdom and the priesthood and the hallowing, even as he promised through the law." The expression "hallowing" has the same meaning as that which later was expressed by the term *Perushim*.

When the attribute "hallowed" is assigned to everyone, it is clearly implied that not only the priests ought to be *Perushim*, but that all of the people were so intended. Pharisaism, *Perishut*, at first only a priestly obligation, was now extended to the whole people. This was done in earnest. Laws of cleanliness and dietary laws, formerly applicable to the priests alone, were made compulsory for all. Here again Pharisaism, which developed side by side with and against the priests, provided the "Oral Law" with its particular field and function, that "Oral Law" which discovered the new by explaining and interpreting the old. The Pharisees claimed not only priestly privileges for themselves, but also priestly duties. And thus the people did away with a large part of what had distinguished the men of the Temple from the general population. This also meant a struggle with the priestly nobility, the Sadducees, and here again synagogue and Temple came in conflict. Hence the basic, or at least the ever-present, element of the conflict between Pharisees and Sadducees was eliminated when the Temple ceased to exist.

Naturally this conflict was most acute during those periods in which the priestly privilege and the importance of the Temple were used as instruments in the struggle for power. Such was the case with the Hellenistic high priests, with their successors in the last generations of Hasmoneans, and finally with those who were, or were supposed to be, the tools of Herod and the Roman procurators when they ruled in their own right or by virtue of their priestly office, and had control over the Temple. It was at this time that the antagonism between the priests and the Pharisees necessarily passed over into enmity, and sometimes into open hostility. It was at this time that what the synagogue cherished as peculiarly its own was more than ever surrounded with a loving zeal. The synagogue belonged entirely to the Pharisees; they were its creation, and their gratitude was expressed in their loyalty to it. It was thanks to them that the destruction of the Second Temple did not create a void in Palestine. With almost revolutionary determination, they enlarged the rights, influence, and dignity of the synagogue, so that it was able to take over the heritage of the Temple. From now on the synagogue was also the Temple; only the Temple sacrifice was lacking, nothing else.

A revolutionary step was in fact implied in the act of Yohanan ben Zakkai, one of the leaders of Pharisaism, who, soon after the Temple went up in flames, not only conceived but actually realized—by virtue of his right of decree, the *Takkanah*—the transference of the essential functions of the Temple to the synagogue. It was almost a revolutionary step when the Day of Atonement—in accordance with the clear edict of the Bible, a day given over to the Temple, the high priest, and the sacrificial service—became a day belonging to the synagogue and its men. It was as though an essential part of some definite law of the "priestly Torah," the Book of Leviticus, a law called there "a law for all time," had been taken out of and transplanted from its clear context. There was something revolutionary in the fact that Simeon ben Yohai, a Pharisee of the following generation, associated the *Shekhinah*, the "dwelling" of God, which in almost every book of the Bible is identified with the Temple, with the synagogue and the house of study. Revolutionary, too, was the declaration that wherever Jews assembled for their devotions and the study of the Torah —wherever they formed a congregation—the Lord was with them, He "dwelt" in their midst, just as He had dwelt in the Temple. It was as though God Himself had been led by His congregation from His old seat, the Temple, into their new house. As revolutionary a change as this was in its fundamentals, it was also, even in its ultimate effects, an almost self-evident consequence of the preceding period. It had been prepared beforehand. The real answer, which accorded with the changed conditions, had already been formulated. It is a sufficient example to point out that even while the Temple was still in existence the priestly blessing was introduced into the synagogue service. The fall of the Temple marked only the external triumph of Pharisaism; the definitive victory had actually already taken place.

But here we may note something odd: the Temple in ruins became in the end more influential than the Temple whole. During the period when it stood, it was always possible to oppose it. Later, when its reality gradually began to dwindle even in memory, it could be reconstructed, so to speak; little by little it became a symbol of the past, and thereby, very soon, a dream of the future. Little by little there arose a romanticism of the sacrificial service, which found its expression in the liturgy. To the generation that experienced the fall of the Temple, Yohanan ben Zakkai declared that Israel now had a means of atonement that was as valuable as the sacrifice—good deeds. Decades later, at the time of Hadrian, Rabbi Jonathan declared likewise that study of the Torah was equal in value to sacrifice and that it was a sacrifice that could be offered any-where. A century later, Yohanan ben Nappaha made a similar statement, as did his colleague, Simeon ben Lakish, who said that he who studied the Torah should be considered the equal of those who performed the sacrificial service, that he was one of those who "serve the Lord, who stand in the house of the Lord." A Babylonian teacher of that time added that he who was well versed in the Torah did not need sacrifices. Gradually, however, the tone changed, and even Yohanan ben Nappaha offers instances of this change. The notion that placed a value on the study of the Torah equal with the performance of the sacrificial service was now somewhat restricted, and only he was praised who studied the rules of the sacrificial service;

he alone was called the equal of those who once performed the sacrifice. But this is all part of the romanticism of a later period.

Furthermore, the Pharisees very quickly inculcated the people with the idea that the old prescriptions regarding the payment of dues to the priests and their assistants, the Levites, should be meticulously observed. Only he was recognized as a *Haver*, i.e., a member of the congregation, of the "brotherhood" or *Hever*—the corresponding Greek term *adelphotes* is also found in the New Testament—who exactly observed these prescriptions; those who evaded them were not thought of as belonging to the congregation and were referred to deprecatingly as *Am ha-Aretz*, "the people of the land." The servants of the Temple and their descendants were not to be deprived of their hereditary means of support. But this was merely an act of loyalty, and it was loyalty less to the Temple itself than to the men who had taken a personal part in its activities. The synagogue of the Pharisees not only survived the Temple externally in the temporal realm but also prevailed over it historically in the realm of ideas.

In addition to the conflict with the Temple, Pharisaism carried the decision in another conflict, that between the community and the state. This conflict did not arise out of the fact that the sacrifice was the official ceremony of the state, while prayer and scriptural recitation constituted the ceremony of the community. It had a deeper reason. Wherever a community is organized as a separate entity within a state, sooner or later an antagonism develops between the two. The community strives to realize in itself an invisible and ideal state, and thus unwittingly turns against the visible state with all its insufficiencies and its political expediency. This is clearly seen in

45

modern times, for instance, in the history of the English Congregationalists and Presbyterians.

At first this antagonism did not exist in Palestine. The commonwealth newly formed in the ancestral land lacked political independence; it was under the domination of great powers. A state seemed to exist, but despite its closed and coherent character, it was really not a state at all; it experienced no political problems and had no political needs. Hence it was able, and was permitted, to consider itself a community only. Moreover, the foreign power did not dictate to and oppress the Palestinian community either too directly or too frequently. The Jews usually felt it to be a protection rather than a restriction. The Persian Empire, to which the new Palestine belonged for the first two centuries of its existence, and likewise in the following century the Egyptian empire of the Ptolemies, intervened directly in the life of the Jewish people only on rare occasions.

This situation changed under the Syrian Seleucids, who for a short time seized the little country for themselves and bitterly oppressed the Jews. And it changed fundamentally in the Hasmonean epoch during the century of independence. Under the Hasmoneans the Jews possessed a state of their own, a state in which they had a personal share, whether for joy or for sorrow, and for which they were responsible. This state was governed by priests; the High Priest was the ruler, and the priestly nobility, the Sadducees, usually enjoyed his trust and held the highest state offices. It was at this time that the antagonism towards the priest received a new emphasis. Now the priestly *regime* was opposed. Conflict with the state was sooner or later bound to break out, and the less the ruling priest, who was the personification of the visible state, conformed to the ideal, the

46

more violent the conflict. The struggle became a lasting one when Herod, a member of the neighboring Idumeans, won the overlordship by cleverly obtaining the favor of the Romans. And it continued afterwards under the Romans themselves, who through their procurators exercised despotic control over the land.

It is certain that the community organized against all these at an early date. In the Sayings of the Fathers, in which the Pharisees after their triumph tried to demonstrate the antiquity and permanence of their tradition, the last member of the Great Assembly, Simeon the Just, and Antigonus of Sokho, who "had received the tradition from him," are followed in the account by five pairs of men considered the further representatives of the tradition: Jose ben Yoezer and Jose ben Yohanan, Joshua ben Perahyah and Nittai the Arbelite, Judah ben Tabbai and Simeon ben Shetah, Shemayah and Avtalyon, who are also mentioned by Josephus, and finally Hillel and Shammai. It is very probable that these men had been the successive heads of the community. The man who closes this series, Hillel, had come from Babylonia in the time of Herod, and, like a second Ezra, taught a new meaning and new interpretation of the Torah, a new Midrash. The community created a dynasty of its own in Hillel's family, a dynasty that traced its origin back to King David and challenged the House of Herod. Hillel passed as the prince of the community, and there is hardly any doubt that the people looked upon him as their secret anti-king, the legitimate ruler opposed to Herod, the usurper. And there is certainly a core of historical truth in the talmudic story of Yohanan ben Zakkai, who before the fall of Jerusalem took good care to save Gamaliel, offspring of his family and the future prince. He was the grandson of that Gamaliel who was the teacher of the apostle Paul.

It is understandable that the Pharisaic community should have striven to win influence in the state. From old writings it is clear that these efforts were predominantly directed towards achieving authority in the Sanhedrin, the highest judicial and administrative body. In any event this was one of the stakes in the political struggle between the Pharisees and Sadducees. This consideration also influenced conflicts that concerned the theory and practice of law. But it was not only a question of influence and authority—something more serious and profound was involved. Pharisaism was more than an organization, it represented a heroic sense of the mission of the Jewish people. And any heroic mission in which a community finds itself joined necessarily passes beyond the limitations imposed by a state. In the eyes of these men the struggle for God and his commandments was often a struggle against the commandments of the state. A comparison with periods closer to us in time, above all with Puritanism, makes this clear. The state is always defined by its interests. Pharisaism was a heroic spiritual attempt to locate the leading principle of the state not in its own interests but in the law of God, the attempt to define the ideal of the state by the community ideal, to build it, as Josephus correctly says, into a "theocracy," the rule of God.

This explains the tremendous sense of expectation and messianic faith that informed these men. The more heroic the imperative, the more passionate their longing and enthusiasm. A theocratic ideal is not—or at least was not at that time—conceivable without a messianic conviction. The tension, the contrast between the ideal and the reality, was too great to make any other solution seem possible other than this heroic one.

Only the Messiah could bring about the ideal state; steadfast faith had to be kept in his coming and his community had to be prepared for him, the community of the "separated," the *Perushim*. The messianic enthusiasm distinguished the Pharisees from the Sadducees, who, the ancient records show, had compromised with the interests of the state. The Pharisees were not always quick to draw the sword, only a few of them were such zealots. But they inflexibly rejected any compromise and called for the exorcism of the "demon" of state interest. And their longing was all the more fervent since—although they could not always regard the existing state as their own—the land was their land, its soil was holy in their eyes, and they wanted to make it a realm of purity, of "separateness." Thus they triumphed over the state, too, triumphed by virtue of their messianic faith; the state disappeared, but they remained, not only as individuals but as a collectivity.

This is Pharisaism. Needless to say, many of its followers—often because of the character of Pharisaism itself—suffered from grave faults. Wherever the "community" opposes the state, or even the church, which resembles the state, a sectarian spirit easily develops, and with it a confined and suffocating atmosphere. We are here familiar with the artificial piety that takes the place of true religiousness and converts it into a kind of exercise, a sport almost. Judaism, in its ancient and its modern form, is also acquainted with this. Wherever an ideal of saintliness is erected, there the sanctimonious are always to be found, the "painted ones," as they are called by the Hasmonean king in the words handed down to us by the Talmud. When religion becomes the subject of popular instruction and is intended to be the possession of the people, it can also degenerate into the mere business of religion, where petty narrow-mindedness is given full scope. All this was present, to be sure, in Pharisaism. If we had not already known this through earlier sources, we should have found it related not only in the Gospels but in the Talmud, as well.

Yet that is not really Pharisaism; it has a different essence. Pharisaism represents a great attempt to achieve the full domination of religion over life, both over the life of the individual and the life of the collectivity; an effort to exalt religion beyond a merely auxiliary role in the life of man, the community, and the state. It took the idea of saintliness in earnest; it responded in deadly earnest to the summons to make life, including daily life, conform to the ideal—the summons in which the Pharisees discovered their function and their justification: " 'Ye shall sanctify yourselves and be holy'—ye shall be *Perushim*." Pharisaism was a heroic effort to prepare the ground for the kingdom of God. The name belongs to the past; the meaning contained in it has remained ideal reality.

TRADITION IN JUDAISM

TRADITION IN JUDAISM *

The spiritual and religious life of Judaism at the beginning of
the Christian Era was determined in its essentials by a permanent tradition of its own. This tradition was comprised first
and foremost of the biblical books. The Holy Scriptures had
been written down, and every scroll and sentence, indeed every
letter in them, was surrounded with the most meticulous care.
As the Torah says, among the Jewish people the Bible was "the
inheritance of the congregation of Jacob" (Deut. 33:4), and
they had always had a grateful awareness of their heritage and
its riches. But at the same time there was the desire not to be
merely the guardian of an inheritance, merely the inheritor of
a valuable possession. Joezer the priest, a teacher of the first
century, characteristically said with regard to the written heritage: "Study the Torah, for it is *not* your inheritance." [1] He
thus expressed what the possession of the Bible among the people had come to mean at that time. It was the book beside which
no other was supposed to exist; it was, indeed, far more than a
book, far more than anything that had ever been written.
Therefore, it was not merely to be read and known, it was to be
rediscovered anew in every word, ever and continually to be
made one's own. Out of the idea of spiritual inheritance was

* A chapter from the book, "The Gospels as a Document in the History of the
Jewish Faith" (*Das Evangelium als Urkunde der jüdischen Glaubensgeschichte*).

created the commandment enjoining the close study of the Bible, so that its truths might be known and spoken rightly. There were many studies and investigations made to find out what was made known and imparted (*maggid ha-katuv, melammed ha-katuv*) in the written word. The word that was read was never merely the complete and final written word, it was also always a spoken word, forever moving and advancing. It always denoted something new. Thus the Bible had a twofold function: it was the written book, the "written teaching," read again and again and copied over; and it was the book revealed and preached by people, the "oral teaching" that was proclaimed over and over again and listened to and handed on. The tradition—never ending, never silent—lived on in the Bible.

When a religious idea was thus discovered in the Bible and presented by a true teacher, it was almost like a revelation from God. For it came from the word of God, deduced from it by one of the masters, one of the pious and wise. All were thus obliged to learn it and guard it. It was especially to be tended by the faith of the scholar, by his will to be carried forward, disseminated, and continued in life. The word was an oral one, and yet in a sense it was one written down and engraved in the memory of the disciple. An inward tie between disciple and teacher, linking each succeeding generation through "the chain of tradition," preserved this reverence and piety. The word *Shemua*, which in the Bible means prophetic understanding and which is also used for that which the disciple has heard from his teacher, has a ring of sacred obligation. Every disciple, as was said then, was supposed to be the "witness" of his teacher—to be able to bear pure, genuine testimony to what his teacher had said. The teacher lived on in his disciples.

"His lips," to quote another saying of that time, "should speak from his grave." [2]

Among the people of Israel the history of religion appeared as a great and centuries-long tradition: "Moses received the Torah on Sinai and handed it down to Joshua; Joshua to the elders; the elders to the prophets; and the prophets handed it down to the men of the Great Assembly." When Paul says: "I received that which I delivered unto you," he intentionally uses the words that introduce the Sayings of the Fathers. Paul thus seeks to make his own that tradition which served as the great guaranty for the Jewish people of that time. Papias, too, characteristically appeals to "the Elders"; in the language of the Jewry of that time, the phrase denoted the first and classical representatives of the tradition. And Papias only describes what is characteristically contained in the Jewish tradition when he reports that Mark "recorded in writing the Lord's words and deeds"; Mark's act embraces the whole Jewish tradition: words and deeds (*amar rabbi* and *maase be-rabbi*). Here the language itself points clearly to the community and identity of these ideas.

Every tradition has a destiny of its own, and the Judaism of those days demonstrates this truth in its own unique fashion. Tradition is entrusted to people and is passed on through human minds and human personalities and is "altered by them." Involuntarily and unconsciously the bearer of tradition puts something of his own personality and his own characteristics, great or small, something of his own hopes, yearnings, and faith, into that which he bears in his memory as the words or deeds of his master. Sometimes a tradition acquires a certain closed and resistant character, as is the case with strictly formulated laws, solemn and symmetrically constructed maxims, or short rhythmical prayers. But where there are no such limitations, or where they lose their strictness in the course of generations, the soul of the bearer of tradition only too easily adds to or subtracts from or alters its content.

The disciple, and then the disciple's disciple, in his love of his teacher strongly identified with him, imagines increasingly that the things he himself thinks and desires were in truth the words and desires of the teacher; and what he found strange or dubious in his teacher he gradually omits from his memory of his teacher's words and ways. It is easier for him to alter and modify that part of the tradition concerned with the ultimate problems of life, because here tradition is joined to the most crucial personal problems. What the disciple inwardly experiences, what has become truth and belief in his soul, must have also been experienced and preached by his master; knowledge and the passing on of knowledge here become a question of destiny.

Moreover, the religious imagination always blazes its own trails. It is forever and involuntarily drawing in new shapes and lines, new colors, brilliance, and richness. The urge to associate ideas and images that exists in every mind, and which was particularly characteristic of the Jewish thinking of that time, weaves a new fabric of thought. Words that are alive in the popular language, sayings, deeds told of great men of the past, and the miracles ascribed to them—somehow in the course of the years and generations all these become part of the memory of the beloved teacher, to whom nothing great and sublime is foreign.

The words of the Bible itself gave free play to this process. For it was read in a special way. On the one hand, even when it described no particular person and no particular event, a definite time and a definite biographical situation were read into the words. These situations had to be invented. Confronted with a nameless prayer of the psalter or a wise proverb, one had to consider who had said it, or about whom it had been said, and the answer was: Adam or Abraham, Jacob or Moses. People wanted to experience the individual, personal element in the words of the Bible.

On the other hand, paradoxically enough, the teaching of the Scriptures was raised above the situation and the time to which it belonged, into the timeless and the absolute, indeed, into the pre-existent and the ideal. Even when it told of what happened to a particular person at a particular time, it was interpreted in the light of eternity. Every story in the Bible not only told something, it also meant something. It did not describe what once was, what came to be and ceased to be; it revealed something permanent, absolute, something that once was and was still, and that despite the change of scene and time remained the same. Each story unfolded a grandiose drama that was performed ever anew; however the masks may change, protagonist and antagonist remain the same.

Thus the boundaries of time, the difference between the days, became blurred; past and present began to coexist. The people's yearnings, cares, anxieties, and hopes were clothed in the garment of the experiences and events of the past as they were reported by history and tradition. And conversely, what had existed in the past received its breath, blood, form, and color from the present life, from present struggle, hope, and anxiety. The old message took a present form; what the Bible told, or what they had heard from previous generations, acquired shape and meaning in the time through which the people lived. Past became present, present became past, centuries were spanned. Men lived in the ideas and persons of the past, and in their own lives the past lived again. Above all, in times of grief and suffering, when what the day brought could only seem meaningless and godless, the day was accounted part of eternity, forever the same. What imagination had begun, faith completed.

All this was possible because the Bible had authority over the Jewish people. It contained the ultimate measure of understanding and knowledge. It was not merely a human work but the revelation of the word of the living God. As the word of God, it was always present, always valid for the future; it was bound to give the answer to today and tomorrow. For "the word of our God shall stand for ever" (Isa. 40:8). Thus, for every day and every problem the word of the Bible had something compelling to say. Whatever happened, whatever was spoken, was subordinated to the word of the Bible, was measured by it, defined in relation to it, judged in its light as genuine or false. The word of the Bible alone could reveal what was real and true. Not in what men's eyes had seen or had not seen, not in what men taught or disputed was the final answer, but only in the word of God. People not only thought and hoped in terms of the Scriptures, they also lived and learned in terms of them, and often in terms of them alone. It is for this reason that the Gospels so frequently conclude with the phrase, ". . . that the scriptures of the prophets might be fulfilled." Therefore, for Paul, the article of faith that means everything to him, the one concerning the expiatory death and resurrection of Jesus, was finally and decisively proved by emphatic reference to the Scriptures: "I delivered unto you . . . that Christ died for our sins *according to the scriptures;* and that he was buried, and that he rose again the third day *according to the scriptures*"

(I Cor. 15:3-4). The word of the Bible was the ultimate measure of reality and history.

In view of this fact, it becomes clearer how contemporary figures were so vividly and personally experienced in biblical figures. Friends and foes of the past became friends and foes of the present, and those of the present became those of the past. It must not be assumed that the name of biblical personalities served merely as a disguise in dangerous days, and that the well-informed were supposed to know who was meant. The reader actually identified the past and the present. He read about Esau or Edom, and he was certain that Rome was referred to; he not only thought so or believed it was suggested, but knew it was so. He read about Balaam and knew that all this, word for word, designated the cunning counselor of his own foes, the false prophet at the gates. To the men who wrote down and to those who read what John said to the congregation at Pergamos: "Thou hast there them that hold the doctrine of Balaam" (Rev. 2:14), or Peter's warning to those who "have forsaken the right way, and are gone astray, following the way of Balaam" (II Pet. 2:15), it was an actual fact that the ancient Balaam had reappeared again to seduce them. When people read about the destruction of the First Temple, they knew that they were thus being prepared for the destruction of the Second Temple; when they read about Nebuchadnezzar, they knew that they were being told about Titus. The speeches of the prophets were truly experienced because they spoke not only of the present, but also *in* the present. They proclaimed and revealed what was actually happening and what that which had happened meant.

What happened each day was thus defined by the word of the Bible; the Bible decided the course of knowledge and preaching. It paved the way for its own elaboration in poetry and prose. Just as the old tales were continually recreated in the Bible, so new tales were continually introduced. Wherever there seemed to be gaps, new stories filled them in, since the word of the Bible had to lack in nothing. And wherever the Bible simply did not contain what the people wanted to find there, they added further stories to complete it. Wherever something was obscure, it was clarified and elucidated. In the same way that the word of the Bible was all-significant, so it had to be all-inclusive, as can be seen in the admonition of Ben Bag Bag, a man of that time: "Turn it [the Torah] and turn it over again, for everything is in it." [3] One was almost *obliged* to say more through it. Every generation, when it perceived in the written and oral tradition what was new and peculiar to itself, was tempted further to shape and reshape the tradition in order to make this newness and peculiarity clearly perceptible there. The Bible pursued its way through the generations, constantly being added to in this creative fashion.

The Bible had already undergone a process of transformation. One need only compare the Books of Samuel and Kings with Chronicles to see how naturally a new form was given to the old matter. For example, let us examine those texts of Samuel and Chronicles that deal with David's wish to build a temple to the Lord:

II Sam. 7:8-14.

Thus saith the Lord of hosts . . . When thy days are fulfilled, and thou shalt sleep with thy fathers, I will set up thy seed after thee, that shall proceed out of thy body, and I will establish his kingdom. He shall build a house for My name, and I will establish the throne of his kingdom for ever. I will be to him for a father, and he shall be to Me for a son.

> But the word of the Lord came to me, saying: Thou hast shed blood abundantly, and hast made great wars; thou shalt not build a house unto My name, because thou hast shed much blood upon the earth in My sight. Behold, a son shall be born to thee, who shall be a man of rest; and I will give him rest from all his enemies round about; for his name shall be Solomon, and I will give peace and quietness unto Israel in his days. He shall build a house for My name; and he shall be to Me for a son, and I will be to him for a father; and I will establish the throne of his kingdom over Israel for ever.

It is clear what the later narrator wanted to convey. While the earlier one only reported the facts, the later one inquired into their reasons and explained them: since David had shed blood, he was not permitted to build the Temple; this honor was given to Solomon because he was a man of peace. What happened here is what most frequently happened: the narrator by whom the story was continued continued to invent and introduce into it new matter.

There are even a greater number and variety of such examples in the old talmudic tradition, the so-called oral law. To choose one instance among many, in addition to Pirke Avot, the Sayings of the Fathers, there is the Avot de-Rabbi Nathan, a text attributed to Rabbi Nathan of the second half of the second century, which contains essential parts of the same material. (In many respects, the parallelism of these two texts resembles that of the Gospels, and can often help to elucidate the latter.) We shall now place them side by side, exhibiting both versions of a sentence we have already quoted, but omitting the numerous Bible verses that are adduced in the second text as evidence:

Moses received the Torah on Sinai and handed it down to Joshua; Joshua to the elders; the elders to the prophets; and the prophets handed it down to the men of the Great Assembly.

Avot de-Rabbi Nathan, 1:2-3

Moses was hallowed by the cloud of divine presence and received the Torah on Sinai. Through Moses the Torah was given on Sinai. The Torah that the Holy One, praised be He, gave to Israel, was given only through Moses; it was granted to Moses to be the messenger between the children of Israel and the Omnipresent. Joshua received it from Moses, the elders from Joshua, the judges from the elders, the prophets from the judges, Haggai, Zechariah, and Malachi received it from the prophets, and the men of the Great Assembly received it from Haggai, Zechariah, and Malachi.

Just as in the above-cited text from Chronicles, so here in Avot, the need to elucidate and to instruct asserts itself as the tradition is passed on. The bearer of the tradition becomes a commentator: Moses' incomparable significance is deliberately stressed by solemn repetition; the judges who were actually Joshua's successors and who were unmentioned by the earlier tradition are here given a place between the elders and the prophets. The break in the succession of the prophets that was caused by the Babylonian Exile is clearly marked in the separate mention that is made of the three prophets who lived after that period.

The different and varied ways in which this continuous process of reinterpretation and re-creation was carried on are to be found in the so-called apocryphal and pseudepigraphical writings that close the gap between the Bible and the oral law. A few examples will illustrate this. The Second Book of Chronicles relates that the sinful King Manasseh humbled himself and repented and prayed unto God, and that all these facts "are written in the history of the seers" (II Chron. 33:18-19). The minds intent upon the study of Bible naturally inquired as to what Manasseh had said in his entreaty, and one student composed "a prayer of Manasseh" based on this sentence from Chronicles. The Book of Jeremiah (29:1) tells of a letter, sent by the prophet, from Jerusalem to the captives in Babylon, containing words of admonition and comfort. But an urgent question arose: Did not Jeremiah also warn against idolatry, which must have tempted the exiles in Babylon, even though the Book of Jeremiah is silent on this matter? Thus an "Epistle of Jeremiah" was composed, and it contains what the pious readers felt was missing. Furthermore, the Book of Jeremiah frequently mentions Baruch ben Neriah, the prophet's trusted disciple. Readers of the Bible wondered whether this man, so close to Jeremiah, did not, in the face of the disasters that marked his time, preach to the people; and various Books of Baruch were thus written down.

This post-biblical literature shows how the urge to complement the Bible was transformed into an inner necessity in serious and threatening days, when the sacred word spoke most sharply and inspiringly. When misfortune impended, when portents announced a coming upheaval, souls thirsty for an answer turned to the events and words of antiquity, trying to discover there a prediction of the present and future; and the desire for solace and certainty inevitably led them to assume that the ancient men of God had had foreknowledge of what now took place and what was to come. Enoch, who "walked with God," and whom "God took," lived before the deluge—

surely he must have known about the new deluge that was approaching? Baruch witnessed the fall of the First Temple—had not his prophetic mind also previsioned a new destruction of Jerusalem, a new burning of the Temple? Ezra had lived through the critical period from the first years of the decline until the Exile—had nothing of the new disaster and the new certainty been revealed to him? Had not these men, in the days through which they lived, grasped the course of the future, had they not prophesied the meaning of all time, of the whole span from the creation to the last day? Thus arose the apocalyptic literature that constitutes an essential part of post-biblical literature, those books of revelation that were attributed to the men of the Bible and that describe with wonderful effect past times and past places, the ups and downs of history, and the Last Day of Judgment. Everything that glimmered—now indistinctly, now significantly—in the obscure words of the Bible, all the traditions and legends of the people concerned with the beginning and the end, the yearnings that stirred in them and the trust upon which they relied, were gathered here. A deep conviction found its expression; dreams, visions, and ecstasies made all these mysteries real to the men who wrote these books. Hence it is that the image always means more than the idea, the envisioned more than the known.

It was first the Bible itself, and then later it was the literature directly following it that supplied the various forms, stylized patterns, outlines, and embellishments that served as models for this creative revision. Thus, there was the life of marvels and miracles, with its temptations and its steadfastness, with its illnesses and healings—we find it in the stories of Daniel, of Judith, and of Tobit. There were the stories of martyrdom in the Book of Daniel and Second Maccabees. There were the tables of ancestors and the records of the generations in the Book of Chronicles. There were the compendiums of sayings in the Book of Proverbs, as well as in Ecclesiastes and the Book of Sirach. There were the prayers and anthems, and the songs praising the words of God and the wisdom of the Psalms. Allegories and maxims that summarized the basic matter of the Bible were known; the people were familiar with them through the oral tradition. Everyone was acquainted with the certain sequence and style of the short prayers, as well as with the type of apocalyptic vision of the last days, above all as it was described in the Book of Daniel. Whatever was said and written, whatever was related, for all its distinctiveness and variety, was set forth traditionally after an old model. The style had been fixed.

Each new creation was more and more predetermined as to its content. All the crucial ideas and hopes that were awakened by a new day were, so to speak, children of the mother Bible. Their core had been fixed from time immemorial. What was the path from creation to the latter days; how the beginning and the end met on this path; the revelation of God's will and its fulfilment; the meaning of suffering, martyrdom, temptation, and ordeal as instruments for raising transient human existence to eternity and truth; the life and passion and triumph of the Messiah when he would come one day in the fulness of time; what would come to pass when the higher world entered into this lower one, when the miraculous kingdom with its messengers descended to this earth—all this had been known for generations, it had all been said once and for all in the Holy Scriptures. Each new period could only repeat, no matter how much it added its own lines and colors to the picture. It was permitted to utter the answer, to elaborate and embellish it, it was perhaps also permitted to interpret it, but one should not devise one's own answer; the only true answer had been established long ago and for all time. What faith, certainty, and hope dealt with and expressed had been written down and clearly established; what it contained was given, traditional, complete. Each day, each experience, had to be interpolated in it; all the distinctiveness and novelty of the present, all the events of the moment, had to be adapted to it. But what was actually taking place could never determine this content. What was any event of the present day compared to what the word of God revealed? What could be the importance of a supposed discovery or an intended refutation as against what the Lord had ordained from the primal beginning to be forever true; what could anyone add or take away from the Holy Scriptures? History could only fulfil what was written there. The Bible, together with the tradition that started from it and returned to it, held the meaning and the message of everything that happened, fixed the way in which the people were instructed in God, man, and the world.

Since the Holy Scriptures were thus the cosmos, comprising all meaning, where every individual detail had its significant place, a particular type of intellectual investigation evolved from it. One might almost say, a particular type of logic. It was a type of thinking that grew neither out of the process of taking apart—analysis—nor out of the process of putting together—synthesis—but out of the process of placing side by side—association. Its keystone was resemblance, analogy. The psychological foundation was an act of recognition; a certain experience reminded a man of a verse in the Bible, and this verse reminded him of another. Thus ideas, words, and events that seemed to be remote from one another were brought together, and inferences were drawn from one to the other. There was a verse in the Bible that described every person one met, a verse that decided the character of every event that happened to one. Resemblance became identity: "This is he that was spoken of" (Matt. 3:3).

A great act of recognition took place again and again; the world and the word were felt as one. The determining idea was that in the Holy Scriptures nothing was accidental, nothing was without meaning and value. The same axiom ruled here that Aristotle invoked to justify reasoning by analogy: "God and nature do nothing in vain." This principle, that of sufficient reason, was here applied to the Bible: it is God's revelation, and God did not say anything, be it the slightest word, without a specific purpose or meaning. Each one of God's words held a secret. The relations existing between these words were thus of the sphere of ultimate knowledge. To rediscover contemporary people and events in the Bible, to set the changing reality of the world by the side of the absolute of the Scriptures, constituted an act of truth-seeking. Thus recognition became a task of the tradition, and the recognized relationships entered the lore. Because the Bible contained the totality of truth, the fate and history embodied in the tradition had to find their way into the Bible.

JUDAISM IN THE CHURCH

JUDAISM IN THE CHURCH

In a twofold sense there is such a thing as a history of Jewish ideas. Jewish ideas have a life and a development within Judaism; but they likewise have their existence outside of Judaism in the general world of ideas. There, too, they are active as a living force, as a leaven; there, too, they create and define changing epochs. Hence there is both a Jewish and a universal history of Judaism.

We can recognize this factor—to give an example near to us in the present—in the history of the various social movements. These movements spring from two sources. On the one side, they are derived from Plato's idea of the mathematical state. The state and its perfect law, in whose infallible power and effect Plato believes, is the instrument with which to shape the proper kind of man and conduct him into virtue and happiness. This the state alone can do; it must therefore be absolute, a dictatorship. The state is accorded a right of unlimited power; over against it, the individual is conceded no right of his own, either of choice or of desire. Plato is the founder of every system based on the idea of hierarchy and the omnipotence of the state. Every secular, every ecclesiastical, as well as every ideological dictatorship, even to the Bolshevism of our own day, has derived from and been nourished by Plato's social ideas and philosophy of the state.

Another, altogether different tendency, which has only the name of socialism in common with this first tendency, has its source in the Bible, in Judaism. Its point of departure is not the state but man, the idea of man as brother and neighbor. Judaism, unlike Plato, who takes a pessimistic view of humanity, has no faith in the state, indeed, but has an optimistic faith in man. For Judaism, man is the strongest reality on earth; the state and the laws of the state acquire goodness only through the agency of the good man. When human beings are brought up in the exercise of mutual love and justice, when each person thinks of his neighbor as a brother, when each person recognizes the rights of his fellows, the social law and the true society will have been realized. "That thy brother may live with thee" (Lev. 25:36)—in this maxim is contained the social idea.

It is possible to trace these two tendencies, the Platonic and the Jewish, through the social movements of the last century, and it is very interesting that Karl Marx, for example, a Jew, goes back to Plato in his socialism, while such Christians as Saint-Simon or Kingsley proceed on the basis of Jewish ideas. Thus a Jewish element is alive in general socialism.

But the real history of Jewish ideas outside Judaism is in the church. Paul, the creator of the Christian church, regarded Judaism and its Bible with conflicting emotions. On the one hand, he regarded the period of Judaism—and in consequence the period of the Bible—as ended. At that time the belief was widespread among the Jews that world history consisted of three epochs: first, the period of chaos—tohubohu; then the period of the Torah, beginning with the revelation on Mount Sinai; and, finally, the hoped-for period of the Messiah.[1] If the latter period had commenced, it necessarily followed that the epoch of Judaism and the Bible had come to its end. In conformity with this, the Gospels say: "Till heaven and earth pass, one jot or one tittle shall in no wise pass from the law, till all be fulfilled" (Matt. 5:18). When all is fulfilled, and the Messiah has come, the period of the law will have come to its close.[2] The law—and for Paul the word "law," as is frequently the case in talmudic literature with the word "Torah," stands for the entire Bible—is for him only the "schoolmaster to bring us unto Christ" (Gal. 3:24). With the Christ began the time of those who had come of age. If, however, Judaism and the Bible still retained their validity, then the Messiah could not have come.

It thus becomes comprehensible why Paul fought against the law with all the determination of his faith, as if it were a life-and-death struggle for his religious existence. And, I repeat, the law meant for him the entire Bible, every commandment in the Bible, and not merely the so-called ritual law. Hence this question for him became one upon which everything turned. If redemption had in fact taken place, if faith and baptism made it manifest, it followed that the law had ceased to exist; if the law were still in force, it was proof that the hoped-for time of fulfilment was not yet at hand. Either the law or redemption! Whoever maintained that the law was still binding was an unbeliever, for he denied the redemption. Hence for Paul it had to be the case that Judaism had ceased to be a religion, either of the present or the future, and the Bible had ceased to be the Bible, that is, the book of the present and the future (Col. 2:14, et seq.; Eph. 2:15).

On the other hand, however, everything that Paul taught and proclaimed, all the proofs of his faith, rested on this selfsame Bible. For him it was the divine revelation of ancient times, it held the promise of the Christ, and it was therefore "holy, and just, and good" (Rom. 7:12, 14). It provided him with all his arguments. From this very book, whose further binding force he contested with the utmost earnestness, he took everything that was the basis of his preaching, everything that he declared to be the significance of the death of the Messiah. Only with the help of the Bible could he prove the fundamental principle of his doctrine. For him the all-decisive phrase was still: "It is written"—written in this book. His whole mode of thought derived from the Bible. This was the same contradiction that informed his entire personality. On the one hand, he announces his freedom and independence from Judaism, and on the other, he continues his pursuit in Judaism of the Jewish mode of thinking and teaching. He had lived so deeply in Judaism that he was never able entirely to escape from it. Whether he wanted to or not, he always found himself back again on Jewish paths of thought. The Jew that he remained in his innermost being throughout his entire life kept up a constant struggle in his soul with the man of the new faith. This is the explanation for the cleavage that is to be found in his preaching as well as in his personality.

Among those who came after Paul and were his disciples, there were many for whom—unlike Paul—a complete consistency was possible, whose opposition to Judaism was not limited by an earlier history. No bond, either of the blood or of the soul, united them with Judaism and they felt their task to be the liberation of the new religion from every Jewish element, leading to the establishment of a pure Paulinism.

There were several ways in which this could be done. One such way, the first, was employed by the author of the Epistle of Barnabas, who lived *circa* 100 C.E., and who is supposed to have come from Egypt. He sought to preserve the Old Testament for Christianity in its character as the foundation of Paul's theology by denying it to Judaism and claiming it entirely for Christianity. Allegorical explanation offered him the means for carrying out this purpose. He uses it constantly in the Old Testament and with its help everything objectionable—that is, everything thoroughly Jewish—is removed, and every present and actual relation to Judaism is eliminated. Every word in the Old Testament acquires a Christian meaning, with the result that the book in its true sense can only be a Christian possession, just as the church in general is said to be the true Israel, the true seed of Abraham. A literal understanding of the Hebrew Bible is in his eyes a Jewish error, worthy of damnation, the work of Satan. The entire Old Testament became an exclusively Paulinian book; only that which is purely Christian is biblical. This method resulted in the additional advantage that Christianity acquired an early history of its own and its beginnings could be traced back to the days of the creation of the world. In contrast, the Jewish people was represented as a people led astray by the devil, a people who in reality had never possessed a covenant with God, to whom a divine revelation had never been given.

And yet this method had its dangers, too. Once the right of interpretation was admitted, at the same time the possibility of each and every kind of interpretation was conceded. If the book was understood in this one allegorical sense, one could claim to understand it in any other allegorical sense, even in the Jewish one. Freedom from this book could be won only by repudiating it entirely. This conclusion the Gnostics drew, especially Marcion. It was they who were in reality the unambiguous and consistent disciples of Paul. They rejected Judaism and its Bible completely. Marcion goes so far that, in order to make this rejection absolute, he explains away as a forgery and a Jewish interpolation everything in the Pauline Epistles that seems to him to be Jewish, everything where a connection between Jesus or Paul and Judaism emerges. For him, only that which is unconditionally opposed to Judaism is true and genuine. In order to establish a pure Paulinism, he revised and corrected the texts of the Gospels and the Epistles. And in order to guard against the possibility that anything Jewish might find its way, through allegory, into his religion, he insisted upon the most literal interpretation of the Old Testament—exactly as did a contemporary of his, the proselyte Aquila, pupil of Rabbi Akiba and translator of the Bible into Greek, who, according to an old report, came from the same city (Sinope) as Marcion, and was his bitterest opponent.

The essential theological basis of this tendency lies in its repudiation of Judaism. In order to separate their Christianity in its origins and entirety from Judaism, in order to have an unambiguous Christianity and a God exclusively their own, the adherents of this view proclaimed an extreme dualism. They taught the existence of a twofold God: the evil, dark, cruel God of the world, the God of Judaism, and the good, pure, spiritual, loving God of Christianity, who is exalted above the world, the God who manifested himself for the first time in Jesus the Christ and who had never before revealed himself. When the Gospels speak of the two trees, of the corrupt tree that bears only corrupt fruits and the good tree that bears only good fruits (Matt. 12:33), nothing else is meant by this than these two opposed divinities—the base God of the Old Testament who creates evil exclusively, who possesses no higher value than the world itself, whose creator and ruler he is, and who will perish at the same time as his heaven and his earth; and the lofty Christian God who brings forth only good and who is without any relation to the world. There is no deeper antithesis than that which exists between these two. For Paul, the God of the Hebrew Bible had been the God of the Christ and his own God; but here, in the gnostic doctrine, the two Gods stand in unbridgeable opposition. The God of the Jews and his book represent the real adversaries; they are the evil principle; all redemption signifies redemption from this world of Judaism. And for this reason the Jews as such are the real enemies of the Christ and the true God. They are the only ones who—all of them together, their patriarchs, their prophets and their teachers—will never be redeemed.

But an inescapable difficulty emerged from such a belief. Once the Hebrew Bible had been abandoned, once everything of a Judaic character had been removed from the Gospels and the Epistles, all that remained were the doctrines of redemption and the sacraments; everything of an ethical character, everything in the nature of a commandment or an obligation had been done away with. Only one choice remained: either a complete libertinism or an absolute asceticism. And so in fact it shortly proved to be.

At first there was a disavowal in practice of all commandments. The principle was here and there made explicit: To him who has been redeemed, to the pure Paulinist, "all things are lawful" (I Cor. 6:12). People felt themselves to be pneumatic, free men of the spirit, and as such many believed that they were beyond good and evil, exalted above morality and chastity, free, bound by no law and no commandment. It is given to him who is exalted above the law not only to recognize God but likewise the "depths of Satan" (Rev. 2:24). For the man of the spirit everything that his body does is after all unreal.

This is the first way of achieving liberation from the law;

Marcion pointed out the second way. For him all earthly existence was something to be put aside at the same time as the law. Corporeal existence was for him *caro stercoribus infersa.*[3] There was only one kind of piety on earth—asceticism, and, ultimately, self-annihilation. He forbade all pleasures of the flesh and insisted on the strictest kind of fasting. He forbade all sexual intercourse, even in marriage. He admitted to the rites of baptism and communion only those who were willing to take the vow of celibacy or who, in case they were already married, would vow to preserve complete sexual separation. According to his verdict, marriage was tantamount to death; the true life is the annihilation of everything corporeal. The struggle against the corporeal is the struggle against the Jewish God of Creation, the struggle *ad destruenda et contemnenda et abominanda opera creatoris.*[4] He who has conquered his corporeal element has won a victory over the God of the Jews. The final goal for which religion exists is the bringing of the race of men on earth to extinction. Once accomplished, the triumph over the Jewish God, the wicked God of Creation, will have been achieved. This was the last consequence of the intention to purge Christianity of its Judaic element.

It is understandable that, for a Christianity which wished to free itself from every trace of Judaism in this way, all life in this world and any relation to the forces of civilization were impossible. The church was obliged to conduct a struggle against Gnosticism if it hoped to establish a domain in this world; and this struggle for its existence became for the church, willing or not, a struggle for the place of the Old Testament in Christianity. This all-important reason was now added to the original historical reasons why the church clung to the Old Testament. The Catholic church was shaped and consolidated in its struggle in behalf of the Old Testament against Gnosticism. It finally carried the day when it succeeded in establishing the position of its Bible, in which the unity of the Old and New Testaments was affirmed and thus the unity of the Jewish and the Christian God.

This was also the time in which the church began to enter into relations with the state—at first simply side by side with it, and then later as its ruler. Two things made it possible for the church to attain this rulership: first, its canonization of the Old Testament, and secondly, and connected with it, its adoption of the Stoic principle of natural law. Natural law and Old Testament law were equated by the Catholic church, a process important in itself and at the same time decisive for the church's future history. What distinguishes the Middle Ages is this equation of the Decalogue and natural law. In consequence, the church was now in a position to develop a doctrine of state and society, and so supplement the pure individualism of its doctrine of salvation and redemption with social features. In this manner the coexistence of church and state and the recognition and utilization by the church of the state were rendered possible.

As a further result of this joining together of the Old and New Testaments, this concession to Judaism, Catholicism was now in a position to achieve a system of ethics. Gnosticism, and especially Marcion's doctrine, had been a religion entirely devoid of ethics, as has already been indicated. And this was in fact the logical Christian point of view, for in principle there was no place for ethics in Paul's system. Ethics had been abandoned because it was a part of the law that had been abrogated by the new justification through faith. Everything was accomplished through the miracle of baptism, through the mystery; everything was fulfilled only through faith. In comparison with this, any good that man did had no real significance. Faith here is the antithesis to ethics. To prize any kind of conduct, even the most moral, and thus to prize the Ten Commandments, is a return to the law beyond which humanity had been led by the Christ. The only choice was one between faith and ethics, the savior and the law. This is the fundamental alternative with which Paul confronts the believer.

As far as Paul himself is concerned, the Jewish element in him was much too strong: he held to a system of ethics; but it was, like his attitude towards the Old Testament in general, the result of a deep inner inconsistency; his conception of faith led him out of Judaism, but in his human character, in his moral feelings and his feeling for the commandments, he remained, afterwards as before, a Jew.

Here, too, where the Jew in him was stronger than the doctrine, he differed from his disciples, who had come out of paganism. They had no bond whatsoever with Judaism. The Epistle of Barnabas was therefore able to say: The tablets of Moses are broken. Among the Nicolaitans in Ephesus and Pergamum, and among "them that hold the doctrine of Balaam" (Rev. 2:14), it would seem that their belief that they had already been redeemed led them to licentiousness and that libertinism of which mention has already been made;[5] among the Cainites, the evildoers of the Bible were held to be examples of men who had achieved redemption.[6] Paul set the ritual and the ethical on the same plane; both were the law; whoever believed himself led forth from the one was able to believe himself exalted above the other.

The church needed the Old Testament's moral code in order to oppose this tendency. It therefore laid down the principle of faith and works, and so acknowledged the right of the Old as well as the New Testament. How compelling the necessity for compromise must have been is apparent, for instance, in the fact that the Epistle of James was taken into the New Testament and placed at the head of the Catholic Epistles. The Epistle of James is nothing other than an inflexible polemic against Paul's principle of justification by faith without the works of the law; it expressly declares that man is justified by works and not by faith alone (Jas. 2:14-26).

The great Catholic doctrine was developed on the basis of this historical compromise with Judaism. It was a compromise, and the Jewish element, understandably, lost much of what was distinctively its own. The one God preached by the prophets was interpreted according to the trinitarian conception developed by the Fathers of the Church. The meaning of the Old Testament was interpreted christologically. In part, biblical law was identified with natural law and so was relegated to the plane of pure nature, in contradistinction to what is inwardly religious. In part, the law was placed on the same level as the religious rites and ceremonies, so that the one as well as the other was considered in the category of good works. But to the extent that Paulinism was obliged to participate in this compromise, it was obliged to circumscribe something of its principle, "by faith alone."

It is understandable that this compromise bore within itself the seed of a perpetual strife. Disagreements were bound to reoccur in the church: now pure Paulinism would attempt to preponderate, and now the Jewish element would attempt to enlarge its scope. From this time forth this spiritual struggle determines the inner development of the church. One thing, to be sure, held firm: the church's doctrine of the Trinity. Here there was hardly any conflict. The Trinity remained a fixed center, even when the so-called doctrine of tritheism (which sought to separate the three persons of the Godhead) was for some time professed alongside the official dogma. But as for faith and works, explanations and counterexplanations soon began to make their appearance. The teachers of the church divided on this problem, so much so that one could say that the history of church dogma is so to speak a history of Judaism within the church. The church experienced its spiritual epochs in the inner alternation of the active, strongly ethical-psychological individual Judaic element with the passive, magico-sacramental faith of Paulinism, where the individual was dissolved into the metaphysical. The historical accomplishment of the papacy, the task that it performed over and over again with great diplomatic art and with still greater spiritual strength through all the antagonisms and conflicts, was the maintenance of the compromise.

That a compromise was involved became apparent soon enough, since works and faith each found its champion in a strong personality, the one in Pelagius, the other in Augustine.

According to Pelagius, the concept of grace has an entirely ethical character and for this reason he reckons the law a part of it, as he in general assumes no essential difference between the Old and New Testaments. He argues the freedom of the will of man, whom God has confronted with the choice of good and evil. He argues that every man, even the non-Christian, can do good, and thus there is salvation even for the unbaptized —in all these things the line of Pelagius' argument is a Judaic one. But with the same determination that Pelagius affirms this doctrine of *liberum arbitrium* and the *possibilitas boni et mali*, Augustine opposes it. Augustine emphatically insists upon the nonexistence of the freedom of the will since the fall of Adam, that since that time man is evil in his nature and under the ban of original sin. For Augustine, grace has an entirely supernatural significance. All things flow from it; man contributes nothing by himself. It chooses some few people without any real reason, and without reason condemns the many to be the great mass doomed to perdition. And this supernatural mercy has its sphere exclusively in the church. Salvation is attained only through baptism by the church—even an infant who dies unbaptized is doomed. Pelagius, in accordance with his doctrine and in agreement with the ancient Jewish teachers, accords men of other faiths or even unbelievers the possibility of good, since virtue itself is a decisive power, and faith also embraces faith in the good. Augustine, however, denies the possibility of virtue in the pagan, and virtue itself is without significance in comparison with the sacrament, since all salvation depends upon the grace upon which it is founded.

The thought of the Catholic Middle Ages fluctuated back and forth between these two poles. The opposition of the Scotists to the Thomists is an illustration of this. (It is interesting in this connection to note that Pelagius and Duns Scotus were both Britons.) Attempts were continually made to effect a compromise between the two extremes. It is only natural, of course, that the church condemned and repudiated Pelagius, yet it always came to terms with a kind of semi-Pelagianism. Augustine, to be sure, was declared a saint; but the church nevertheless resolutely repudiated pure Augustinianism, even when it was revived by such important Catholic personalities as Jansen and the members of the Port-Royal circle. It retained the compromise of the early church, this combination of Paulinism and a Jewish element, even though the influence of the former was always preponderant.

With Luther and the Reformation, the passage was made

from compromise to open attack; war was declared on everything not Paulinian or Augustinian. In one point Luther, to be sure, reverted to Judaism: in the idea of the priesthood of all believers. Even in this the Catholic church had created a mediating doctrine: it had made a distinction between the inner priesthood in which all the baptized were included and the external priesthood of only the ordained.[7] On this point Luther's inclination, at least in his early, revolutionary years, is towards Judaism. With the idea of the priesthood of all believers a new chapter in the history of Jewish doctrine in Christianity began.

In general, however, Luther approached much more closely to the antithesis of Judaism—to a pure Paulinism. He professes a doctrine of unlimited original sin and the complete effectiveness of grace, in the face of which only a purely passive attitude is possible to the believer. Luther arrived at this point through his longing after the absolute certainty of salvation. Inasmuch as Catholicism had demanded works as well as faith from man, and man is never able to perform all these works, the believer, never knowing to what extent grace had been granted him, could hope for salvation, but never could be certain of it. In order to attain this certainty, Luther, like Paul and Augustine before him, denied the value of works and all human activity and made everything exclusively dependent on grace and the faith in it—*sola gratia, sola fide*. In order to maintain his faith unshaken, he had to relegate the commandments to the realm of insignificance. He was obliged to consider a belief in the religious value of moral conduct as impiety, a sin against the Holy Spirit. In place of the Catholic principle of faith and works, the old antithesis re-emerges: either faith or works, or, otherwise expressed, either faith or ethics. Accordingly, all striving, even of the highest and noblest kind, to attain by itself what is good and righteous is nothing other than the path to perdition. Salvation comes from faith alone, which for Luther means faith apart from any moral action. Thus everything of a Jewish character was eliminated from his doctrine.

But Luther went the same way as Paul's generation had gone. As asceticism and libertinism had once followed from the principle that everything depended on faith alone, so now among Luther's followers there emerged both an ascetic tendency and an antinomian tendency that undertook to brush aside all law.[8] Just as the early church had been obliged to make room for works if it was to exist within the state, so Luther soon saw himself obliged to do the same when he began, under the protection of the state, to lay the foundation of his church. Luther extricated himself from this difficulty by a simple but very questionable expedient—he took the moral commandments out of the province of religion proper and relegated them to a purely civil sphere, handing them over and subordinating them to the police and disciplinary powers of the state authorities. Morality is here essentially what the appointed authorities require. It has nothing at all to do with religion proper; at best, it is an appendage to religion. In this way man is inwardly divided, so to speak, into two spheres: the sphere of the spiritual man, who has faith, and the sphere of civil man, who keeps the commandments. This is the un-Jewish feature of Luther's religion, and in this consists its—religious as well as ethical—weakness. Lutheranism was never able to create a real system of *religious* ethics. The state was more and more regarded as the supreme authority over the church, and thus as the lord and master of morality. And thus the state was accorded a position of unlimited power.

In contrast, Calvinism's great historical contribution consists in the restoration to moral activity of the wide scope required of it in Judaism. Calvinism, of course, diverged from Judaism both in its doctrine of the Trinity and in its inflexible dogma of predestination; nevertheless, there is a decided reversion to Judaism in its emphasis on the significance of human behavior, the moral commandments, and the will of God. And even the idea of predestination was more and more moralized in Calvinism. Right conduct becomes the sign of God's election. Man is chosen when he conceives his task to be the acceptance of God's will as his own, the perfecting of the world, the devoting of his life and labor and the life and labor of his neighbor to the service of that which is moral and good, when he labors on earth for the praise and the honor of God. Calvin's faith, unlike Luther's, does not contain the meaning and goal in itself; its aim is to effect the decision to lead a moral existence. The old Jewish idea of the covenant between God and man and, together with it, the Judaic idea of the commandments and the social decrees—everything that we are accustomed to call the "law" in Judaism—all this increasingly suffuses Calvinism. Religion must manifest itself every day in life, it must occupy the most serious and important place in the fulfilment of existence. Calvinism, unlike Lutheranism, is a religion not of moral passivity but of moral activity; it requires the individual to prove himself morally. Hence the Old Testament has an added weight and importance in the Calvinist Bible.

In Calvinism, as in Judaism, the idea of the law is joined with the messianic conception. Wherever the commandment makes its appearance, wherever the demand is made that a place for the good be prepared on earth, that the kingdom of God be founded through the conduct of man, there the messianic idea is awakened—this faith in the final fulfilment of the good, this faith in the true and future lordship of God on earth. This Jewish idea seized hold of the English Puritans in the course of their struggle against godlessness and despotism; this idea guided the Presbyterians when they journeyed westward to found the states of New England. As in Judaism, so here, it is apparent how much devotion to the law and messianic devotion are interrelated.

With Paul, messianic longing had forfeited its essential features. Since he believed that the Messiah had already come and that salvation was a present possession, the idea of a great hope directed towards the future had lost much of its meaning. Now and then, however, the old messianic idea reawakened not only in the early church but even in the church of the Middle Ages. Particularly in times of oppression this Jewish expectation of the coming age of God's rule and eternal peace came to life (*evangelium aeternum* and the *millenium*). The church always detected something revolutionary in this and fought against it with all the means at its disposal. This idea first became a historical religious possibility within the church with the Baptist movement, from which, as well as from Calvinism, sprang that dynamic force which transformed the religious thinking of the United States and England.

The Baptist movement's refusal on principle to tie itself in any way to the state, as Catholicism and Protestantism had done, made possible its unhindered development. Instead, it established a type of free congregation in which it was intended to realize the religious ideal. This new freedom led neither to libertinism nor antinomianism because it did not grow out of an antagonism to the law. On the contrary, it led to the reawakening of biblical socialism, a biblical ideal of holiness, since it tended entirely towards the Jewish idea of the commandment. The Baptists could be Independent and Congregationalist because they placed ethics above the remission of sins and the moral commandment above the doctrine of justification. With this emphasis on the ethical was joined a disinclination to the sacraments and an effort to take away much of their importance. In this, too, we can clearly recognize a turning away from Paulinism in the direction of Judaism. The Baptist movement represents a far-reaching revolution in the role of Judaism within the church. In the England of Cromwell and the America of the Pilgrim Fathers, it passed onto a world-historical plane. Although—or perhaps because—it never ended up in a church, it became one of the most vital religious movements of recent times.

All these efforts at reform have one feature in common: the question of grace and law, faith and works, is the decisive one. Other issues recede into the background. Objections to the doctrine of the Trinity had already been raised in the Baptist movement: Ludwig Hatzer had denied the divinity of Jesus. This question, which has so deeply divided Christianity and Judaism, came to the fore for the first time in Socinianism. It is the first Unitarian tendency in Christianity, and thus the first instance of a turning towards Judaism as regards the conception of the deity. It, too, grew out of Pelagian ideas. These ideas were reawakened in the age of Humanism, when an increasing emphasis was laid both on human rights and on the course of human liberty and action—that is, on the ethical and messianic. The humanists disputed the doctrines of original sin and justification through faith in order to assign the ethical and messianic responsibility to the individual. In consequence, pure dogma was more and more discarded, a plainer interpretation of the Bible was made, and there was an increasing tendency away from christology and trinitarianism in the direction of a strict conception of the oneness of God. A return, that is, was made to Judaism. Socinianism is an attempt at a humanistic renaissance of Christianity, rather than at a dogmatic reformation.

As far as its outer history is concerned, Socinianism enjoyed only a brief term of life. It founded a church of its own in Poland, to be sure, where it only too soon succumbed to reaction, so completely that no trace of it there was left. It was only in Transylvania that a group of congregations were able to maintain their existence through the centuries, despite the persecutions to which they were subjected and despite the conversion—through sabbatianism—of some of their members to Judaism. Although here and almost everywhere in Europe the power and resistance of the old dogma proved victorious, Socinian ideas were nonetheless widely disseminated. Together with Baptism they sowed seeds that came to fruition in later times. In the Netherlands, above all in England, where these ideas won over such a man as Milton, and then in America, they were a powerful impulse to theological thought and undogmatic piety. They represented a fertile Jewish influence on the life of the church. The Unitarianism of a Priestly, a Channing, a Parker, a Longfellow, and a Martineau goes back to these Socinian seeds.

Everywhere in Protestantism throughout the generations this inclination towards Judaism is in some way apparent. What has remained of the old ecclesiastical dogma in modern Protestantism? The Trinity has become more and more often a mere word; the Holy Spirit is hardly any longer an actual divine person, the Paraclete; rather, it represents a sort of spiritual process—it has acquired a Jewish character. The divinity of Jesus, to be sure, is widely considered as dogma in modern Protestantism. But just because of this, more often than not it only signifies a theological concept that is more or less deprived of any content in the course of its dialectical manipulations and ends up in Jewish monotheism. Similarly, the ancient dualism of the church that divided the world into two great realms, that of grace and the son of God, and that of original sin and the devil, has disappeared. Who now speaks of this dogma? How much more do we speak of the religion of entire peoples, of the religious experience of nations, using almost the same terms used by the Jewish prophets? And, finally, the doctrine of faith has gradually reached a position akin to the Jewish doctrine of the moral act and the moral will that lead man to God. Now faith is considered moral faith, and in the end this means Jewish faith. Most of the forms of modern Protestantism point out a way that leads from the early church in the direction of the spiritual and religious realm of Judaism. To be sure, there are ideas in German Protestantism, most of them of an anti-semitic inspiration, that, like the ideas of Marcion, would blot everything Jewish out of Christianity. The history of the church has shown what there remains of Christianity when it has been purged of everything Jewish.

Thus, when we look back over the centuries, we can perceive a history of Jewish ideas in the church. Every change in the spiritual and religious life of the church was basically the taking of a stand with respect to these ideas. Inside and out of the church, Judaism has a lasting life. It can be fought against and it can be forced to give ground, but now, as it did then, it will spring back with new vigor. *Et inclinata resurget*—"And if it is bowed down, it only rises up again."

THE ORIGIN
OF JEWISH MYSTICISM

THE ORIGIN
OF JEWISH MYSTICISM

——

Jewish mysticism is generally designated by the term Kabbalah. In talmudic literature, this term, which probably at first meant "instruction" or "instructive speech," is used to denote the books of the Prophets and the Hagiographa as distinguished from the Pentateuch. It was only in the post-talmudic, so-called gaonic period, that the term Kabbalah came to mean the oral tradition, and it is in this sense that it is later used as the specific name for Jewish mysticism.

To say that the Jewish mystical doctrines were not committed to writing but were handed down orally is not, indeed, to say what it is that peculiarly characterizes them. The period in which Jewish mysticism began to take shape was a period of several centuries during which the Jewish people of Palestine consciously and deliberately refrained from writing. The Talmud, the only work composed during these centuries of literary abstention, owes its existence to the fear that its content might be forgotten, rather than to any literary compulsion. Moreover, the Talmud is the book of a school, rather than of a definite personality. Its first section, the Mishnah, is a record of laws more than it is a literary work; and its second section, the Gemara, is not, properly speaking, a book directly written down, but is a compilation.

It is extraordinary that a people endowed with such great literary powers, a people that had written one book after another, now seemed to impose upon itself an ascetic determination not to write. For it was that—not a loss of ability but a refusal, not a dwindling of power but a deliberate resolve. This decision was parallel to the deliberate renunciation of creative power in the realm of sculpture and painting. Just as the Jews, in the name of the one God, the pure spirit without form or image, obeyed the commandment: "Thou shalt have no other gods before Me. Thou shalt not make unto thee a graven image, nor any manner of likeness, of any thing," so, for the sake of the one Book they now imposed upon themselves the obligation not to have any other books before it. If a new word may be coined, monotheism was now joined with monobiblism: the rejection of more than one book corresponded to the rejection of more than one God. Even when the Mishnah and Gemara were committed to writing, the fiction that there was only one book was maintained; the Talmud was held to be part of it, to be nothing but the old Torah.

Just as monotheistic determination erected a definite boundary against other religions, so this rejection of books was intended as a protection against the dangers of the growth of sects. In every new thought or utterance, the Jews consciously returned to their original tradition. We can follow in detail how, with the establishment of the Bible and the struggle for its recognition, this repugnance to new writings asserted itself. This was done for the Bible's sake, and a high price was paid for it. For a talent that is blocked, an organ that is no longer used, loses its powers. As a result of the decision not to write books the literary gifts of the Jews were considerably impaired for a long time. The old creative powers continued to operate only in the sharply coined and easily transmissible maxims and epigrams and, above all, in the marvelous Hebrew liturgical poetry of the first centuries C. E.

Thus it is not a distinguishing characteristic of the Jewish mysticism of that period that there is no book or literary monument to bear witness to it, that it is older than its books. On the contrary, the first book that was actually written down, later on, is a mystical book. It was, to be sure, considered secret doctrine; in the Mishnah (Hagigah II, 1) we read that it is forbidden to speak of the syzygial doctrine of the male and female principles (*Arayot*) before three persons; of that which was before the creation of the world (*Maaseh Bereshit*) before two persons; and of the beyond, the world of the vision of God's throne (*Merkavah*), even before one, unless he is a sage capable of apprehending it by the power of his own mind. Something of this secret, magical quality has always surrounded Kabbalah. But the reason for not committing it to writing was not that it was supposed to be esoteric; as we have said, when the place of the Bible had been finally secured and there was a place again for other books, the mystical book was the first to be written down. The real reason was much more this general one, that it sprang from an age which rejected all books. Hence the mystical doctrines for a long time were transmitted only orally, and were kabbalistic in the medieval sense of this term —were, that is, oral lore.

Thus the original form of the Kabbalah is lost in the uncertainty of an unrecorded tradition. Nevertheless, its content is discernible. In order to characterize it, some general considerations must be kept in mind. There is no such thing as mysticism pure and simple; every religion develops its particular mysticism according to its particular character. We must deal

95

not with mysticism in general, but with the mysticism of Buddhism, Taoism, Neoplatonism, Judaism, Christianity, or Islam. It goes without saying that all the various mystical tendencies have something in common, namely, the attempt to establish a direct connection between mutable man and the eternal infinite being, to admit man into the realm of eternal being. Whether the meditation aiming at oneness with God is predominantly pious or speculative in character, whether it constitutes a predominantly emotional or spiritual absorption, whether its background is more or less characterized by philosophy or by *pia ignorantia,* is of secondary importance.

The characteristic feature of mysticism is always the experience of, or the faith in, the possibility of completely conquering the distance between man and the beyond. It is this immediacy that must be stressed. For mysticism in the proper sense of the term does not exist where the connection with the absolute is mediated, be it by a sacrament, an exercise, or a rite. Where this is the case, one cannot speak of mysticism, but only of a mystery cult. Conversely, the distinctive characteristic of mysticism is this very attempt to become one with the absolute. Whether this absolute is conceived atheistically, or pantheistically, or as a personal God, whether the value of personality is ascribed to man or denied him, is not important in a consideration of mysticism as such. These differences or particularities are determined only by the religion or philosophy within which a given mysticism develops, and it is through these different religions or philosophies that mysticism has acquired its various historical forms.

Jewish mysticism can be explained only when the premises and specific nature of the Jewish religion are taken into account. What distinguishes prophetic religion, the basis of

Judaism, is its ethical character. The piety that is demanded of man is identical with moral action; he must acquire his religion through his life, which he shapes. All faith is grounded in this, and all knowledge of God is associated with it. The paths leading to God are those of the good deed. Therein lies the strength, the effective power of this piety, but by the same token its field of action is the human world, this earth. The Jewish religion holds man fast to earth; this earth becomes his world, which is the domain of piety.

It is also the origin and starting point of Jewish mysticism. For this mysticism is intended to raise man and his piety above the earth, to lift him above the terrestrial realm into the universe, to make ethical man a cosmic being as well. Man's piety must not remain only on this earth, it must find its domain and its answer in the vastness of the universe. The same cosmic problem gave rise to Jewish mysticism that in the beginning of Christianity led to the transformation of the figure of the Messiah into the Christ of the Epistles to the Ephesians and Colossians. Jewish mysticism was governed by the same need that governed the transformation of the historical Messiah into the Messiah whose place and significance are cosmic. It was precisely in the messianic doctrine that this had its starting point, for it was the figure of the Messiah, as well as the related figure of primordial man, *Adam Kadmon,* that provided a certain easy transition from the ethical to the cosmic.

However diverse the periods of Jewish mysticism, all of them have this in common—that they represent an attempt to transform the man of this earth into a creature of the universe, the man of the commandments into a cosmic being. Yet in Jewish mysticism it is always this earthly creature that *is* the cosmic man. In other words, this earth is not negated, man is not detached or delivered from it; instead, his earth is placed within a great cosmic system. Access to the cosmos, and thereby access to the creative power of God, is opened to man. And this implies that the earth remains the point of departure and that the task given to man on this earth, the ethical task, is still postulated. The specific feature of Jewish mysticism is precisely that it never ceases to be ethical. The connecting paths of its cosmos are ethical, all the forces of the world are forces of will, forces for the fulfilment of the commandment. Ethics is here extended into the cosmos. Man remains a man of this earth, and the highest destination of this earth is to become cosmic through him, and thus become directly connected with the realm of perfection, with the universe, which, for the non-mystic, is only the world of the beyond.

Man's personality, together with all the duties that are laid upon him, is thus preserved. Jewish mysticism is never release from will or a release from self; on the contrary it is a doctrine of the most intense moral activity, of the creative powers of man who fulfils the commandment with all his heart. This distinctive feature of Jewish mysticism is expressed in the fact that at a later period the same term, *Kavvanah,* denoted both devotion—that is to say, the spiritual attitude of the man who fulfils the commandment with all his heart—and the mystical absorption through which man wins access to God.

For the same reason Jewish mysticism is not pantheistic. The strict theistic faith in a personal God to whom man appeals and prays is fully preserved. God and the world are never identified; the world is not absorbed in God, or God in the world. What distinguishes Jewish mysticism is rather that it enlarges man by bringing him into relation with the many worlds of the universe, so that the effect of his action reaches the infinite, so that his ethical act also becomes a cosmic act and he discovers a path towards the realm of universal creation. One might designate this feature of Jewish mysticism as its pananthropism. This raising of man into the cosmic while his ethical character is fully preserved, this extension of the scope of his action into the infinite, characterizes all the phases of Jewish mysticism.

Its beginnings, if the mystical-sounding passages in the Wisdom of Solomon and especially certain texts of Philo are disregarded, go back to the first century c.e. We find it here both as ecstatic mysticism, as "the state of being outside," to use a significant phrase of the Talmud, and as speculative mysticism. As we have said, the goals of its search are existence before creation, then the pleroma, or fulness of divine excellences and powers, and, finally, the syzygies, or pairs of aeons. Both the ecstatic and speculative methods are intended to reveal all this to man, to make him share in a revelation in which he is transported beyond the bounds of this earth into the divine mystery which is the truth, to the immediate proximity of God. At first, all this appears alien on Jewish soil, and, in fact, it must be traced back to the influence of Gnosticism, a mixture of Greek and Oriental mythologies and religions, which at that time flowered in the countries surrounding Palestine. The ideas concerning the cosmos with which Jewish thinking was confronted had to be dealt with, refuted or accepted, and it is out of this need that the Jewish mystical movement arose, although its premises existed within Judaism itself.

The oldest testimonies suggest that the leaders of the people were at first not unfriendly to these experiences and doctrines, even though they strove to confine their dissemination to a chosen few. It is interesting to note what is reported about

Yohanan ben Zakkai, the first head of the rabbinical school after the destruction of the Temple, and Eleazar ben Arakh, his disciple. In the Palestinian Talmud (Hagigah 77a), we read: "It came to pass that Rabban Yohanan set out traveling on a mule, and Rabbi Eleazar ben Arakh walked behind him. The latter said to him, 'Teach me a section of the *Merkavah.*' And he answered, 'Have not the sages said that a man shall not expound the *Merkavah* even to one person unless he is a sage and has the knowledge of it himself?' Then Eleazar said, 'Rabbi, permit me to speak a word of it before you.' And he answered, 'Speak.' When Rabbi Eleazar began to expound the *Merkavah,* Rabban Yohanan descended from his mule, and said, 'It is not fit that I should hear someone speak of the glory of my Creator while I am riding on a mule.' Then they sat down under a tree. And fire came down from heaven and ringed them, and angels danced around them, joyful as wedding guests before the groom, and an angel called from the fire, 'Truly, these are the secrets of the *Merkavah.*' Thereupon all the trees opened their mouths and sang anthems, and thus what was written was fulfilled: 'And the trees of the forest exulted' (Ps. 96:12). When Eleazar finished, Rabban Yohanan rose, kissed him upon the head, and said, 'Praised be the Lord, the God of Abraham, Isaac, and Jacob, who gave our father Abraham a wise son able to expound the glory of our Father in heaven!' " [1] There could be no greater praise than that given by the words, "to expound the glory of God"—and these words are used here to describe mystical speculation.

However, at an early date this mysticism began to be viewed with suspicion. Concerning four teachers of the generation following that of Yohanan ben Zakkai, we read in the Palestinian Talmud (Hagigah 77b) as follows: "Four men entered Para-

dise [that is, the place where one is in the presence of God]—
Ben Zoma, Ben Azzai, Aher, and Rabbi Akiba. Ben Zoma
looked and died; Ben Azzai looked and went mad; Aher destroyed the shoots [that is, he caused defection among the
youth]; and Rabbi Akiba entered in peace and left in peace."
This is meant to indicate that he abjured mysticism. The warning contained in this passage was later codified in the Mishnah
(Hagigah II, 1): "He who speculates about four things would
fare better if he had not been born—about that which is above,
about that which is below, about that which was before, and
about that which shall be after. He who thus diminishes the
glory of his Creator would fare better if he had not been born."
Thus, mystical speculation is now described as "diminishing
the glory of God."

Between Yohanan ben Zakkai's words of highest praise and
the verdict of the Mishnah lies a historical interval during
which theosophic mysticism was rejected in the realization of
the dangers with which mysticism could threaten what was distinctive in Jewish doctrine.[2] Then the following words of res-
ignation were said: "The Torah is like two paths, one of fire
and one of snow. He who takes the first, dies in fire; he who
takes the second, dies in snow. What should he do? Let him
take the middle path!"—the middle path between the mystical
and the rational.[3]

However, one essential mystical element was preserved in
this epoch in an idea that was particularly close to the thinking
of the time: the idea of the *Shekhinah*, or earthly presence
(dwelling) of God. In the old biblical conception, the seat of
the *Shekhinah* was the Ark of the Covenant and later the
Temple. After the destruction of the Temple, a new solution
was called for. Just as the divine service became dissociated

from the Temple, so the idea of *Shekhinah* had to become independent of it. This was explicitly formulated by the teachers of the generation following the destruction of the Temple. They declared (Avot, III, 2 *et seq.*) that where the Torah was, the *Shekhinah* was, and that when men turned to the Torah, the *Shekhinah* was among them. One of these teachers did not hesitate to apply a classical passage concerning the *Shekhinah* in the sanctuary—"in every place where I cause My name to be mentioned I will come unto thee, and bless thee" (Exod. 20:21)—to the man of the Torah; the man of the Torah became the sanctuary. In particular, Simeon ben Yohai gave this idea various formulations: where the synagogue and the house of study is, there is the *Shekhinah*; wherever the people of the synagogue and house of study wander, the *Shekhinah* follows them. The seat of the Torah was thus given a cosmic significance—it was the place where man is directly connected with God. This was the starting point of the mysticism of the Torah, and with it the mysticism of the synagogue and house of study. In later times, this idea had a rich development in Judaism.

The oldest mystical writings in existence, however, relate to those other forms of mysticism of which the Talmud informs us, and which (again probably under the influence of the thought of the surrounding world) reasserted themselves: the ecstatic and theosophic-speculative forms. They are usually records of visions. These visions are partly of a purely literary character, in the manner of many old apocalypses and ascensions, colorful visions to which the saying of the Talmud (Tosefta, Megillah IV, 28) that "many expounded the *Merkavah* but never beheld it," may be applied. But part of them also represent—and this has usually gone unnoticed—documents of genuine ecstatic experiences, real states of rapture. What the authors of these writings relate, they had seen and heard in their transports; all the extraordinary words and images they use express what they experienced through their senses. This is especially true of the so-called *Yorde Merkavah*, the men who attained the *Merkavah*, whose visions have been preserved in the so-called *Hekhalot* writings, intended to describe the *Hekhalot*, or heavenly porticos.

The Jews at that time also had a certain technique for achieving ecstasy. The Gaon Hai, head of the school of Pumbeditha, who lived *circa* 1000 C.E., reports as something well known that "many scholars were of the opinion that there are ways to achieve this for a man who, thanks to certain qualities, is able to strive to behold the *Merkavah* and to cast a glance into the porticos of the heavenly beings. He should fast on certain days, put his head between his knees, and whisper into the earth many songs and hymns exactly as they are written. Thereupon he beholds the inside and the porticos; it comes to pass as though he were seeing these seven porticos with his own eyes, and it is as though he stepped from one portico into another and saw everything that is in them." [4]

The *Hekhalot* writings contain a peculiarly poetic element; their hymns influenced the liturgy, and, above all, the prayer mysticism of later times—the belief in the "mystery of the prayer," in the ecstasy that carries the man who prays from the earth to the seat of God's glory, the belief in the cosmic effect of the prayer, in its capacity for opening and closing the gates of fate.

At about the same time as these *Hekhalot* writings there was composed the *Sefer Yetzirah*, or "Book of the Creation," in which theosophic mysticism, the philosophy of cosmic man, found its first literary formulation. It represents the first attempt to create a philosophical terminology of mysticism through the free formation of words. This terminology clearly suggests the influence of the Neopythagorean and Neoplatonic philosophers, particularly that of Proclus. The basic idea of the book is that man is capable of discovering the secret of the Creation. According to it, the Creation is the work of the Creative Word, and the word is built of letters. They, like the primal numbers or spheres, are the elements of everything; they constitute the elementary relations, the laws. He who by virtue of the true faith that leads him to God knows how to combine them correctly and order them, as it was given to Abraham in his covenant with God, knows and determines the laws of the universe; he has become a cosmic being, something like Laplace's spirit. God reveals his law, his covenant, to the man who has attained Him through faith.

With the *Hekhalot* writings and the *Sefer Yetzirah*, the earliest period of Jewish mysticism is completed. Everything contained in its subsequent rich history has its origin here. The characteristic feature of this subsequent history is the increasing emphasis on the ethical element. Despite all its bizarre, theosophic, and artificial traits, this mysticism is increasingly associated with man's will and the idea of founding God's sanctuary on earth. It teaches a history of the world which is that of the pious and the just on this earth. To them it is given, as was previously said in the Talmud, to connect God with earth, to find a path to Him through the spheres, and to pave the way for his advent and rule. The energies of the world are here identified with ethical forces; the pious act of complete immersion in the good leads to the *unio mystica*. Mysticism retains the commandment.

As a result, an increasingly intense longing for the future

entered this mysticism. It acquired a messianic tone. Its aim was not to release man from will and from the world, but to reconcile human will and the world with God, and to bring the beyond down to this earth, to transform the Sabbath, to whose poetry all its love is directed, into the breath of the world, into the life and fulfilment of mankind. This challenging, imperative, active, messianic element, this emphasis on personality and on the idea of the future, which is nevertheless combined with immersion in the bliss of peace, in the mystery of the Sabbath, became the distinctive feature of Jewish mysticism. And this evolution is the result of the distinctive nature of Judaism itself.

GREEK AND JEWISH
PREACHING

GREEK AND JEWISH
PREACHING

—

It is a characteristic phenomenon in intellectual history that related ideas sometimes appear independently of one another in different places at the same time. It often seems as if the Creator's hand had strewn the same ideas about the earth.

Perhaps the most striking instance of this is the variety of the forms of prophecy in the two and a half centuries of Israel's history beginning with Elijah and ending with the return from the Babylonian Exile. This was the same period during which the whole great culture area of Asia and Europe gave evidence of great religious fertility. In India there arose the masters of the Upanishads and, following them, Gautama Buddha; in Persia, the authors of the Gathas, Zoroaster and his disciples; in China, Lao-Tse and Kung-Tse. And above all in Greece it was the epoch of religious growth and striving, the period of the thinkers and poets who attempted to rise up to the conception of the new divinity. Many of them were philosophers as far as the form of their exposition is concerned, but in their aspirations they were really in search of a new religion.

The paths of development of the ancient religious cultures are also largely parallel. The words of almost all these men were written down, and the classical religious literature thus

109

created had soon to be supplemented by commentaries, exhortations and edifying discourses. A specific type of teaching evolved; it no longer proclaimed a new truth but aimed at expounding and spreading the truth already proclaimed. The prophets who saw divine visions and hearkened to voices from above were succeeded by the interpreters who possessed their books; the seers and their disciples were succeeded by the preachers—for the term "sermon" ought properly to be applied not to prophetic utterance but only to this subsequent and derivative type of eloquence.

The sermon, this new type of discourse, had as many forms as the different ideas of faith that it expressed. Among the people of the Zoroastrian faith it took the form of homiletic explanations of old mysterious religious sayings, the Gathas, and of expositions of the Vendidad, or law. We also find it in Indian Buddhism; the Suttanipata lists among the most precious "Mangalas," or gifts of life, together with reverence and modesty, contentment and gratitude: listening to didactic lectures at a meet time. We find it in China, too, where it became a regular feature of religious life. But we find it above all in the great cultural area of Greece. Freudenthal, one of the greatest Hellenists, denied the existence of the sermon in the Greek world and saw in it a specifically Jewish phenomenon.[1] His too-narrow conception of Greek religion and the sermon led him to this view.

The Greek religion and, even more markedly, the Roman religion, were officially state religions of the ancient type; they appealed to the individual only in his capacity as citizen; as an individual and a personality he received nothing from them. As a citizen of the state he was obliged to participate in the religious rites; and so long as he participated, the state was usually tolerant of everything else. His religious ideas and theological conceptions remained a matter of indifference. That is why the Epicureans and the Skeptics found it so easy to live in peace with the state and the state religion. And that is also why the foreigner was given many concessions not granted to the citizen. A passage in a speech against Andocides, ascribed to Lysias, characteristically describes an offense against the state shrines as a real crime only if it was perpetrated by a native.[2] The state religion, τὸ πάτριον, as the Greeks called it, or *civilis religio*, as it was termed by Varro, is concerned only with the nation, it provides and asks for a national cult only.

Whatever religious needs, apart from the domestic customs, the individual felt, could be gratified only either in the mystery cults that promised him redemption and apotheosis, or in the philosophical religions that aimed at answering his doubts and showing a path for his will. In the period of the decline of the ancient world, the more man separated himself inwardly from the state and learned to look on himself as a citizen of the world—Philo's remark that the νόμινος ἀνήρ is a κοσμοπόλιτος expresses the mood of the times—the more the mystery cult with its miracles, on the one hand, and philosophy with its general view of the universe and man, on the other, were bound to win over the people. For the attempt to bolster up the tottering ancient beliefs by the doctrine of the dual truth, such as was made at the end of antiquity by the Skeptics and in the Middle Ages by the Nominalists, could offer only a temporary way out of the predicament. It did not change the fact that individual religion was either that which philosophy provided or the mystery cult.

Hence it is at this point alone that we must look for the

111

sermon; for it is not addressed to the citizen, but to the individual, the believer. The sermon is alien to the mystery cult, to be sure; for this cult does not appeal to reason and will but speaks exclusively to the imagination and the sensibility; most important in it is the dramatic enactment of the death of the god and the sacramental sacrifice. Thus the sermon could find a place only in the philosophical religion.

This is especially true of the Cynico-Stoic religion, the most successful and beneficent in the realm of Greek culture. It has many recorded sermons, as well as a variety of oft-described preachers. There were those who were true to their calling, and those false to it; those who were dominated by their moral conviction, and those who relied on their technical skill and only sought applause; the pulpit orators to whom the community came, and the wandering preachers who went to the community and attempted to catch its attention by means of striking witticisms or a drastic rhetoric. These men elaborated at an early date the sermonic oration with its rules —this was the diatribe or, as it is also called, the dialexis or homily. These terms literally signify speech and counter-speech, discussion; the opposing views were presented, each with its proof and arguments, and then just as thoroughly refuted. They maintained the fiction that the preacher whom no one ever contradicts was nevertheless obliged to meet continual contradiction.

At that time there was a widespread need for the sermon. Each of the various schools possessed a truth that its adherents religiously believed in; philosophy had here and there acquired an almost dogmatic character. This truth needed to be explained and propagated. In this respect, the democratic feature given it by Socrates played a determining role. He it was who had declared that virtue and piety could be learned; that is, they were accessible to everyone and therefore could and should be preached. This tendency of Socratic philosophy, which was followed not so much by Plato and Aristotle as by the Cynics, is perhaps its most particular contribution to Greek thinking. It was the opposite of the kind of exclusive doctrine proclaimed by Heraclitus or Pythagoras and poetically expounded by Pindar, according to which virtue was not accessible to everyone, but was a gift of the gods to the elect.

The same democratic feature—one might almost say, the same Socratic manner—characterizes Judaism. Here, too, we have the postulate that religion can be learned. It is the Torah, the "teaching." This term implies that it is open to and designed for everyone; that it is to be preached to all men. There can hardly be a more universal term. The Torah is thus opposed to the Gnosis, the knowledge derived through the sacraments, which man acquires not by his own efforts but receives only if he is among the initiated and redeemed, the science that cannot be taught but only attested, that needs the herald more than the preacher.

Thus Judaism and Hellenism, in virtue of a common didacticism, coincided. The Greeks enjoyed an advantage over the Jews in one respect; they had the formal brilliance and elegance of style that centuries of practice in all the oratorical arts had developed. This was an advantage, but it was also a danger. All too soon rhetoric provided an opportunity for, and in the end demanded, the dominance of the hollow and pretentious conventional phrase, and this often resulted in the sacrifice of real content and conviction. Eloquence was cultivated for the sake of eloquence. It has justly been said that Hellenism died in the cult of beautiful form.

Among the Jewish people this virtuosity was opposed by certain spiritual characteristics and by certain characteristics of the language. The old sermons from the regions in which Hebrew was spoken, or, more accurately, the tables of contents and fragments of sermons which have come down to us in our Midrashim, display what seems to be an almost studied indifference to artistic form. Only interpolated sayings are given literary polish. But the Jews possessed something uniquely their own that gave all their sermons an inner coherence. They possessed unity of religion and the unity derived from a basic religious book, while the Greeks had unity only within each school and with regard to each particular doctrine. And in addition to this there was the great importance of the living oral tradition as against the rigid texts, expressed by the term Midrash—absence of dogmatism, the right, yes, the obligation to explore the Bible and to bring forth from it and form religious ideas.

Such intellectual self-assertion has often been required in the course of history, and so it was at that time. It was necessary to take a clear position in respect to ideas that advanced the claims of the opponents of Judaism or, which were even more dangerous, ideas claiming an affinity with it. And the surrounding Greek world was by no means the most insignificant source of these ideas; they sorely tried the convictions not only of Alexandrian Jewry, as is often supposed, but of Palestinian Jewry as well. The distinction drawn between the native and the Egyptian communities has importance as a classification rather than as a mark of essential difference. On the old Jewish soil, too, there took place that specific interaction in

114

which the West and the East—especially since the days of Zeno, son of Manasse, the founder of the Stoa—everywhere sought to ally themselves anew. All this can still be followed in the ancient Hebrew sermons, and it shows that the Jews of that time did not try to evade the spiritual issues of their day.

All the different paths by which Greek philosophy penetrated the Jewish world can no longer be distinguished. It is not necessary to assume a close familiarity on the part of the Jews with the particular Greek works. Many themes and tenets, Platonic, Stoic or Epicurean, were at that time part and parcel of Greek culture and were carried with it everywhere. The Greek wandering preachers were doubtless well known in Palestine at that time; Greek, too, were probably those "philosophers" of whose disputes with certain elder scribes the Talmud often tells us. We know that Greek theatrical troupes had been traveling throughout Asia Minor for many decades; the itinerant orators must have followed these roads even more frequently. The Jewish sermon was therefore referred to by the same term that designated the Greek one.[3]

Whatever their path of penetration may have been, the Greek doctrines were known in Palestine, and native Jewish preaching had to take them into account, either by rejecting or accepting them. For the Jews did not scruple at using the contributions of the Hellenic world, and characteristically enough, they particularly welcomed Platonic ideas, the most ideal of them all. This tendency is well known as regards Alexandrian literature; considering Philo's personality it is not surprising that he should elucidate and sublimate God's words to Moses in such a way that God is made to express Platonic ideas quite explicitly.[4] But in the Palestinian Haggadah, too, we find essentially the same phenomenon. Many examples could be cited and we shall mention at least one of them, because it strikingly illustrates the familiarity the real Palestinian preachers enjoyed with Philo's methods.

In several sermons the revelation experienced by Abraham is described by the following image, emphasizing the lofty and miraculous character of this event: "The Bible says that God led out Abraham. This should be interpreted in the following way: God led Abraham up above the vault of heaven where the Lord dwells, so that beneath his feet he beheld the paths of the stars, the ways and the laws that had been laid down from the beginning." [5] Those who know Plato's *Phaedrus* will be immediately reminded, word for word, of the marvelous allegory in which this greatest of all the Greek "visionaries" describes the ascent of the immortals at the moment when they "know": "For the immortals, when they are at the end of their course, go forth and stand upon the outside of heaven, and the revolution of the spheres carries them round, and they behold the things beyond . . . In the revolution [the divine intelligence] beholds justice, and temperance, and knowledge absolute . . . in existence absolute." [6] The Jewish preacher used the Platonic allegory to describe, in the language of the Bible, what he held to be the most sublime of all experiences, the prophetic revelation.

The same sermon also introduces us into a conflict of ideas, for it adds that God said to Abraham: "He who is beneath the stars, bound up in the earthly, fears them; he who rises above them, into eternity, fears them not. You can be a prophet, you need not be an astrologer." [7]

We see here the cognition of God opposed to astrology, and this opposition preoccupied men's minds at that time, when no science seemed as compelling as astronomy with its concomit-

116

ant astrological fatalism. The ancient idea of fate that was implicit in Greek and Oriental mythology and alone made it supportable seemed now to be elevated to the rank of a science. Jewish thinking, too, although fundamentally unmythical, was influenced by this current to a certain extent; even though aversion and inclination alternated, the impression it made was a strong one. We can follow the process in the apocryphal and Hellenistic writings: the astrological past is introduced into biblical history; the men of God appear now as masters of this art and now as victors over it.

Within the area of Greek culture this science of fate triumphed along with the renaissance of the ancient religion, which occurred at a moment when this religion seemed at an end and which prolonged its life for generations. The moving spirit in this was chiefly Poseidonius, whose importance cannot be overestimated. In him Greek antiquity found once again a spirited religious mind, a mind that attempted to comprehend everything aesthetically, a poet of the cosmos and at the same time a master of language who wrote in an individual style. His influence was wide and lasting; moreover, he exerted it directly and practically in his capacity as teacher of the Roman aristocracy and defender of its political ideas. He affected Jewish Hellenisticism as well. He built a scientific religion out of the old and new, making it possible for an enlightened man to believe in the gods. And thus he became a spiritual power, a power that demanded that one be either for or against. In the cosmogony that he created for that purpose he introduced astrology; the stars became the mathematical proof of polytheism.

Judaism was thus confronted with a changed and more dangerous opponent. For many generations the old paganism

117

and its idolatry had been considered inferior; its gods were futile and inane, the object of a scorn that Isaiah expressed and that was later imitated in the Wisdom of Solomon. But now the belief in the gods reappeared under the sign of science, and the old defense against it was no longer adequate; new weapons and new tactics were needed. This new conflict stirred the Jewish world for centuries, and even longer afterwards there were scars and marks to testify to the existence of a redoubtable adversary who to some extent had even ensnared the victor in his own ideas.

The sermon quoted above, which calls upon the people to choose between the prophet and the astrologer, ushers us into this period. Abraham is presented as one who has achieved faith in God and thereby elevated himself above the orbits of the stars. "In Israel no star has power," this sermon concludes, [8] and with this declaration, which became a principle, the astrological doctrine of fate was rejected.

It is noteworthy that it was with the above-quoted words of Plato that this doctrine was opposed. The feature of his philosophy in which Jewish thinking discovered a kinship is this transcendental impulse, this conception of the world as symbol, and of Ideas as perfect and eternal archetypes of the imperfect and changing world. In a sermon dating from the fourth century we find a sentence that is a direct or indirect transposition of a saying of Philo, or perhaps, also, of Plotinus, who revived Platonism: "The image of the eternal light is the ball of the sun, the image of eternal wisdom is the Torah." [9] Here we have formulated in almost epigrammatic fashion why there was a tendency to interpret Judaism platonically.

And not least of all, a common ground with Platonism was

118

found in the biblical doctrine of man's likeness to God; here again we can observe a characteristic feature that helps us to understand the range of vision of Jewish preaching at that time. The Greek translators of the Bible render the word "likeness" by εἰκών. This term was taken up in the language of the Hebrew sermons, where it denotes man, and in Hebrew texts this Hebrew word is explicitly used to refer to man as the εἰκών of God.[10] The significance of this is not merely linguistic, it is much more religious; there is a deliberate emphasis here, a solemn expression of opposition to other faiths. For in the contemporary religious idiom of the Greek, εἰκών denoted something exclusive. Not every man was the image of God, only the elect were so, who were raised up to the level of the gods. The term belonged to the cult of ruler and heroes prevailing in the Greco-Roman world. Thus, in the famous inscription on the Rosetta stone, whose trilinguality made possible the deciphering of Egyptian hieroglyphics, King Ptolemy is celebrated as the "Living εἰκών of Zeus." The language of this cult was later used in the Christian descriptions of the savior, and among other attributes of the ruler, this one, too, the divine εἰκών, was given to the god-man, Christ (II Cor. 4:4; Col. 1:15). If we recall the meaning of this term in such contexts, we realize the significance of the fact that in Jewish sermons it is used to denote man. Man is given the attribute that elsewhere is given only to the elect of the elect, be it the emperor or god incarnate; here man as such is the εἰκών of God. Thus the specific contribution of Judaism is preserved.

The foregoing remarks are intended only as illustrations of the role of Jewish preaching on the intellectual battlefield of that period. One can fully understand it only if one understands the character of the struggle it conducted. Then one can also understand its style, a style utterly unrhetorical because it expresses the constantly renewed struggle for self-assertion. Hence also its searching and restless quality, which often gives the impression of instability; these old preachers continually sought to find the truth, to discover new paths in the old revelation, paths leading to the present. As it was then, so it remained later, even though in many constricted periods the search moved in circles and was transformed into a game. But the Jewish people always found their way back to the wider expanses and proved their right to spiritual existence in face of the challenge of each new day. Judaism seldom remained in a state of intellectual quiescence; it lacked the necessary consummated religious system that has been proven and proclaimed once and for all. The Jews always strove after religious philosophy rather than after dogmatism; for them principles were more important than results. They could be tolerant of and almost indifferent to the mode of expression because they were always sure of the principle; it always stood firm. Although they lacked the sense of power that comes with success, they had in its place the consciousness of conviction.

And this, both philosophically and historically, defines the present task. It seems a truism to say that he who wants to preach a religion must know it, but it would be well if it were a truism. What is meant here is not knowledge in the sense of knowledge acquired—every honest preacher experiences the fact that he learns while teaching, that he speaks above all to himself. What is meant is knowledge in the sense of a constant searching, which one knows can never reach its end. The first task of preaching is to grasp the meaning of Judaism; here, too, learning must precede technique.

120

A frequent defect of Jewish preaching—and we must not deceive ourselves about it—is that it does not well up out of a sufficiently profound immersion in Judaism. Its roots are often too superficial, they go no deeper than the traditional or the recently invented phrase, the phrase of yesterday or today; its roots are in an outworn, emasculated pathos. Preachers repeat habitual phrases until they themselves are convinced by them; and for those who have no ideas of their own, since they long to be solemn too, there is a last but ready resort to artificial emotion; they attempt to arouse tears by mournfully tinkling their rhetorical bells. *Corruptio optimi pessima* goes the Latin saying. Judaism expresses this in the form of an imperative: "Thou shalt not take the name of the Lord, thy God, in vain!"

The preacher is entrusted with the dignity of his religion; his awareness of this ought to sharpen his conscience. He ought never to forget that his tradition derives from the Holy Scriptures. The soul receives its office only through the commandment, which does not speak of pleasing, but of teaching and elevating. This, of course, requires, in addition to a clear understanding, an honorable character; only a man inwardly free can preach. To fulfil this task is not easy. It is easier to fall off, and then, following the law of gravity, be led steadily downwards. All of us are doubtless subject to moments of half-heartedness when we listen to the counsel of inertia and selfishness, and when everything perhaps sounds indifferently alike. But then let each and everyone recall Virgil's admonition to Dante in the *Divine Comedy*, when the Italian poet in his weariness wants to listen to the advice of worldly people: *Vien' dietro a me, e lascia dir le genti*—"Come to the heights with me, and let men talk." And, after all, to be able to respect oneself and the words one addresses to the community, is a happiness that compensates for many things.

The history of Jewish preaching, too, shows how we can remain faithful to what is best and most characteristic in Judaism. To preach means "to learn and to teach."

TWO WORLD VIEWS COMPARED

TWO WORLD VIEWS COMPARED

———

One thing is decisive in Greek thinking—and it is this think-ing that formed the Western mind—at least since the time it became philosophy: the idea of the work of art. Man, in his in-tellectual and psychical fear of the mutable, that ocean of noth-ingness, took refuge in this idea; it was a fear analogous to that which prompted the Egyptians to mummify the body in an effort to make it endure. The sensual eye that beholds the world around it is only able to possess the instant, and therefore, as Heraclitus and the Eleatics taught, really possesses nothing. It beholds non-being, for only the ebb and flow reach it, and it sees only something that it will never see again. Such an expe-rience does not disclose the thing or person in itself; it merely goes from one evanescent instant to another, it drifts about in the ever-changing moments that die as soon as they are born. Only in the work of art, it was felt, can one discover that bliss-ful land of the always-the-same; in it is manifested the realm of meaning, of duration, of pure form and personality.

Here one of the aims of cognition is indicated; for when the artist, the intuitive thinker, contemplates and creates, he does not grasp and achieve the instant that soon falls back into noth-ingness, but receives and gives the permanent and one, the essence, the thing in itself, which always remains the same. In sensual experience, the casual and shadowlike drift of things passes us by; the work of art confronts us with what is truly seen, because it is always seen: authentic reality, the thing itself, being as such, ὄντως ὄν οὐσία, or, in the words of Plato, the true form, the εἶδος or Idea. This is perhaps the best explanation of the Platonic Idea: it is the work of art, the statue of reality; the Platonic heaven is the temple of these statues. In the work of art, in the Idea, change and mutability are transcended; fear of the evanescent gives place to certainty and calm. Here one of mankind's great thoughts has its awakening.

Only the work of art *is;* only the work of art is true. Greek thought so completely accepts this proposition that it also inverts it: all being, all truth, is a work of art. To discover and grasp being, one must penetrate the work of art.

Hence Greek thought is characterized by a broad unity of science and art, by the aesthetic cast and the aesthetic mood of all cognition. Mathematics and logic are fundamentally the same as music and plastic art; and all of them are philosophy. All of them give us true being, the permanent and the timeless. Numbers, which for us express and determine movement and harmony, are here static, almost statuesque. The laws of the spheres are these static rhythms, this music of the spheres. The description of philosophy as "the sublimest music" given in *Phaedo* is not meant merely as a poetic simile; and when Aristotle celebrates poetry as "more profound and more philosophical than history," he does not mean merely what Count Keyserling says in his book on Schopenhauer, namely, that "every great poem represents the sublation of the empirical in the idea"; for Aristotle, only the work of art is the truth. The concept, the number, the law, the geometric figure, the harmony, the statue, or whatever name is given to it, is always essentially the same: it is always the work of art, the Idea, Being. Therefore, the concept is not, as it is for us, a means; it is an end—the actual goal of cognition; and the same applies to numbers. Whether the instrument is the artist's chisel or the dialectician's logic, both are equally revelatory of the Idea, of Being. The beautiful, the logical, and the mathematical are identical; he who has one, has the others. The philosopher, or lover of wisdom, is also the lover of beauty.

Hence also the unity of cognition and intuition. Reason intuits the concept; it contemplates justice, prudence, science—and this again is not merely a simile. And, for the same reason, there is also unity of Logos and Eros. The Platonic Eros is an experience of the mind and the soul by which man comes to know the always-the-same through the work of art; it is the experience of the magnetism and attraction of the work of art and the spiritual and intellectual raptness it occasions. It is identical with the experience through which the world of concepts grasps and holds the thinker. Dialectics is essentially the same as the erotic. This is most strikingly expressed by a passage in Aristotle's *Metaphysics* in which there is discussed the harmony of the spheres and the way in which the spheres are moved by the supreme Idea—that supreme work of art, that divinity which moves and is itself unmoved. The Prime Mover, says Aristotle, itself unmoving, moves the constellations and the spheres by being beloved of them—in other words, by the Eros that dwells in them, and Aristotle could just as well have said: by its being contemplated by them, conceived of by them. This later led to Dante's doctrine of "the love that moves the sun and the other stars." This Platonic love is less a grasping than a being-grasped.

The Ethos has the same identity with the Eros as the Logos.

The highest virtue, the highest perfection, is contemplation and thought, the love for the highest, the being-attracted, the being-seized, that spiritually unites man with the beautiful, the good, and the true. Ethics, as Greek thinking understood this term, is not what we understand by it—something unconditionally imperative, urgent, dynamic—rather is it something intrinsically aesthetic and intellectual, contemplative and reflective, the contemplation of and reflection on being and the eternal, the concept, the law, the work of art. To quote Aristotle once again: "Contemplation is, of all activities, the most pleasurable and best"; intellectual activity is aesthetically and ethically the most valuable. The term "ethos" means here only: place, attitude, position; the ideal ethical personality is the fixed star. In the realm of ethics, too, the idea of the work of art is the determining one.

The same is true of all manifestations of being. There is a world of being, of the beautiful, the true and the good, there is one cosmos, and all spiritual connections with it, those of the Logos, the Eros, the Ethos, of dialectics, mathematics, music, and ethics, of philosophy and of love, are relations to the work of art; they constitute that type of intellectual contemplation for which the mind itself is a work of art and can contemplate itself by thought, and so know itself. Only when due credit is given to this characteristic of Greek philosophy do we discover the meaning of the Eleatic-Platonic-Aristotelian philosophy, which is the true Greek philosophy; for Heraclitus played the role of the devil's advocate, presenting his arguments only to be refuted, and Democritus never really played a part in this philosophy. Greek philosophy is the apotheosis of the work of art.

This has another all-important implication. Being as a work

of art is perfect, closed. It is beyond all possibility of becoming otherwise, of developing; it remains what it is. *It is consummated.* It is perfect, and therefore complete; and as something complete, it belongs to the past. Interestingly enough, the Latin word *perfectus* denotes all these three meanings: completed, past, and perfect. Every work of art represents something past, a persisting past, yet a past. Properly speaking, there is only one kind of thing wholly consummated—the work of art; to quote Schopenhauer again, art "is always at its goal." Nothing is left to man but to behold it, to think it, to be seized by it, to admire it, and to become absorbed in it. The idea of the work of art thus leads to the idea of consummation as the ultimate decisive answer; in it the meaning of everything is given. The beautiful, that eternalized instant, that present moment which has become the final end, has absorbed the true and the good, and Eros, for whom the instant becomes perpetuity, has absorbed the Logos and the Ethos.

In this One, all thinking, all cognition, all knowledge, is resolved. For us, the term cognition has a connotation of mastering, overcoming, conquering; the Greek Gnosis is veiled in the peace of perfection. Man's spiritual goal and destination lie in the realm of the contemplation of perfection, whether it is the perfection of the cosmos, of a definitive system, of the sublimest idea, or of the sated and unmoving Divinity. Cognition becomes contemplation, and man, engaged in the process of cognition, is locked in the stasis of perfection. Contemplation is always ultimate; it is something absolutely achieved, a past-present after which there cannot be anything further, any future. If Greek thinking is so rich in a sense of possession, so rich in the certainty of its goal, and so poor in illusions, it is also poor in any attempts to go beyond and to see beyond, poor in enthusiasm and passion, platonic, one might say; and the positive and negative aspects of this thinking are implied in its domination by the idea of final perfection.

Above all, this idea determines the positive and negative aspects of Greek ethics. The ideal that it proposes to man is that of ἀταραξία, imperturbability, the attitude of the consummated man to the consummated world. The task of ethics is to make this idea explicit, and the task of man is to represent this work of art. The sage lives his life by offering it up to the contemplation of his fellows; man is conceived of as a work of art, or, in the characteristic words of the Stoa, a spectacle for gods and men. *Ecce homo!* To what extent the figure of Jesus in the Gospel according to John has the lineaments of the Greek sage is shown in the fact that his life is "offered up" (both to sacrifice and contemplation); as has been justly observed, the figure of Jesus has a statue-like character. It does not move man by the force of its imperative, it "moves by being beloved." And the manner, so strange to us, in which in the late Greek period the ideal person and the ideal concept are interchanged for one another and become one in the dogma—the Logos becoming a person, and the person the Logos, and even the Number becoming a person and the person the Number—is based on this idea of the finished and the perfect. The perfected personality is no longer a man but a concept, an idea.

Thus finality, pastness, becomes the ideal, or, expressed negatively, the ideal is future-less. Properly speaking, it is unethical, at least in the sense in which we conceive ethics, in the sense of an impulse towards the new and coming, which is clearly in contrast to what the Greek world conceived to be supreme and to the—one might almost say—cult attitude towards the closed, completed, and definitive ideal. Here ethics

130

becomes contemplation, whether it applies to God or to man, and man thus becomes a god; and because of this, ethics ceases to be ethics. The life of the Greek sage was fulfilled in immobile religious contemplation; he first contemplates and is finally himself contemplated. Life is first the subject and finally the object of Greek religious ethics. Contemplation became adoration. And for the demands of the day and the state, there remained only the Aristotelian doctrine of correctness, of the middle course, or the Platonic state dictatorship, that Bolshevism of antiquity. And in conjunction with all this there is sophistry, the expression of that temper of mind which seeks out the shifting element in things, that artistry of logic and ethics which, in denying finality, gradually denies everything and becomes nihilism. The tendency towards a universal nihilism—political, ethical, and spiritual—always has its inception in the idea of finality.

This idea more and more became the complete answer for Greek antiquity because it was arrived at by still another means: not only by the Apollonian contemplation of the work of art, but also by the Dionysiac-Orphic mystery of the beyond; not only by means of that aesthetic rationalism already discussed, but just as much by means of the empiricism of the religious experience. It was to this that the individual turned with his religious demands, the individual to whom the state religion gave nothing and who was unable to fathom philosophy, and here he found the beyond and its miracles. The mystery permitted him to contemplate the rise from the underworld to the light of eternity, and in the trance and rapture that it gave the faithful devotee, it carried him into that miracle, so that it became his miracle. At first only the beholder of the drama, he soon became its object. When seized by the trance, the mo-

ment became for him fulfilment and finality; something ultimate, signifying permanent possession and eternity, became
his share. From a creature of change and mutability he became
an enduring being, a man redeemed and complete, possessed
of everything. The experience took possession of him; and he
who undergoes it has at the very beginning reached the goal,
the beginning is for him the end. Moreover, the mystery cults
in which West and East at that time discovered each other contained the faith in a divine power of grace that enters man
through the sacrament, frees him from his earthly chains, and
makes him divine; and associated with it was the faith in a predestination that gave man the whole, the beginning-and-end,
that either elects or dooms him. Already Diogenes the Cynic,
the anti-Platonist and adversary of the mysteries, had scorn-
fully pointed out that "an Agesilaus and an Epaminondas, because they were not initiated in the mysteries, are supposed to
dwell in the underworld among the reprobates, while the most
insignificant wretch is given a dwelling on the isle of the blessed
only because he was a mystic." He who has the mystery, whoever he may be, has the certainty of final things.

In this world of mystery the experience of redemption is
everything. It is its Eros, which here has absorbed the Logos
and Ethos so completely that it demands the *sacrificium intel-
lectus* and the *sacrificium voluntatis*. All experience of redemption is psychologically the release from will and the release from reason, the release from everything gradual, from
all limitations, from all struggle and activity. It is a sinking
into the sea of an all-significant emotion, submergence in the
mood in which reality dissolves, in the intoxicating sensation
that releases appearance and being from their finite limits—
the release from life through the subjective experience. Think-

132

ing is pushed back behind emotion and the dreams, the deed gives way to rapture and absorption: Gnosis here signifies redemption and Ethos faith. Life dissolves into instants of experience, consummated moments; it is only in them that the "I" receives its meaning, only in them that it gains a sense of the ultimate, of fulfilment. And for the commonplace daily world, for "the vacuum between the instants," to use a term of Kierkegaard, there remain, besides enthusiasm and that rapture-seeking longing after excitation, the fixed precept, the dogma and the fixed morality with its catalogue of virtues. The flight from the world of change becomes the flight from life into the world of subjective experience—the apotheosis of the instant.

The mystery cult based on subjective experience and the philosophy based on the notion of the work of art represent the two great tendencies in the spiritual and religious life of Greek antiquity. In the end they were able to merge because they have an essential feature in common: both live in the possession of what is fixed and final, in the certainty of having it and being it. Contemplation and rapture belong together—the one had ultimate visions, the other ultimate emotions. Even for Plato the one led to the other, but in his case it was only a mutual attraction. They first merged when the church conquered Hellenism, and Hellenism the church. This came to pass under the sign of Platonism. Plato is the father of the church teachers, not only because his state supplied the blueprint for the real structure of the church, but even more so because the church was able to rediscover its mystery in Plato's philosophy. In the church the two paths became one. Philosophy and the subjective experience, the Gnosis and the sacrament, were synthesized in the certainty of the absolute and consummated man, the redeemer and the redeemed. The two became one: the mystery as work of art and the work of art as mystery. In this synthesis Greek antiquity found its ultimate fulfilment and its end. It died in it, died wearily because its ideal had no future. But the alliance had been concluded and it was lasting. It survived in the church, indeed it survived through the church; it asserted itself because the church most profoundly and most intimately united the two directions; in the church it triumphed over nations and centuries. The great epoch of the church, the Middle Ages, belongs to it.

Throughout the centuries, all its creations are determined by this synthesis. So-called Scholasticism—and Melanchthon, for instance, is still a Scholastic—is the philosophy of finality, the philosophy of concepts that are end-points, answers that are premises. Its faith is in the conclusion, the pre-established syllogism; it deduces final things. Its logic, with marvelous consistency, is the logic of the middle term; the results are known in advance and are presented as the given point of departure; it has only to supply the needed axioms and proofs. All its movement in all the subtlety and richness of its dialectics always takes place in the same space, always in the middle. It does not build; its art is the art of the locksmith: it only shows how to open all the doors to the house of truth, which stands already erected from the foundations to the roof. It can prove everything; for the truth is final, truth is dogma, and only what is final is true. And here, too, in conjunction with this, we have the artist, the skeptic, and the sophist, the busy sophist who finds his realm in the doctrine of the dual truth and dual morality.

Truth is fixed because it speaks of the fixed world. Here the world is presented as the mystical work of art of the *trina machina rerum*—the three-storeyed edifice of heaven, earth,

134

and hell, and that other work of art which is the mystery of the Trinity floats above it. This world contains the pyramid of the consummated state and the consummated church. The prototype above has its image below, the macrocosm has its microcosm. Everything is given beforehand, permanent, all history is history fulfilled, time completed; what occurs in the future is re-occurrence. Only finality is true and real; the devil has his seat in the becoming, and it must be overthrown. And to man it is given only to contemplate, experience, and acknowledge all this, this final answer, this synthesis of the work of art and the mystery; his task is to harbor faith—that medieval Eros—to be seized by it and moved by it, and to be aware in it that he who has it is himself consummated, redeemed. The characteristic feature of the Middle Ages is the unity of the work of art and the mystery, of metaphysics and the symbol, or, in psychological terms, of dialectics and rapture. Here the logician is the devotee and the devotee is the logician, the scholastic is the worshipper, and the artist, he who contemplates, is the dialectician. St. Thomas Aquinas speaks in Dante's *Paradise*. The term *kultus* perhaps expresses most adequately this medieval synthesis of adoration, contemplation and yearning. In it, Eros completely absorbs the Logos and the Ethos; the world is immersed in it. The Middle Ages is the Great Cult with all its miracles and splendor, the Cult as meaning and goal of heaven and earth. It denotes everything and signifies everything, it is the answer and the appearance, it yields up the mystery and the work of art. Rapture and redemption, contemplation and grace, are one in it; Eros, faith, is nourished by it. In it, the idea of consummation, of perfection, finds its ultimate and all-embracing world. Here it became an epoch.

For this reason the Middle Ages came to an end at the point where this idea was undermined. The opposition to it came from two sides. First, and this can be only briefly mentioned here, from mathematics. When Kepler replaced the heavenly spheres, that ancient idea of the perfect, by the planetary ellipses—a deed no less decisive in man's conception of the cosmos than that of Copernicus—and when Descartes supplanted Euclid's contained and motionless geometry with analytical geometry, a new epoch began in the history of knowledge. Statics, in which even the infinite is static, increasingly gave place to dynamics, and the consummated work of art to the function. However, the strongest, most important counter-pressure came from another realm, a realm that the church had absorbed and that it thought it had enclosed in its system of finality—the Old Testament. The new astronomy and mathematics on the one hand, and the rediscovered world of the Old Testament on the other, shattered one epoch and paved the way for another.

If we come to the Old Testament from Greek antiquity and the Middle Ages, it is as though we are entering a different world. We leave the temple of Ideas and the house of the cult and enter the world of life, the struggle of Ethos and Pathos; from the cosmos of being we come into the becoming that wants to be a cosmos, from the enclosed space we emerge upon the endless path. And at first it seems that we are stepping from rest to unrest, from the imperturbability of ataraxia and adoration into a whirlpool of searching and struggling, from the assured seat of final things to the long road that leads to the never-attained goal. Paul had felt this opposition most profoundly and most tormentingly, and it was from it that he fled to the fixed world of unchanging perfection, which is actually

136

its opposite. In the Old Testament every creative idea is the counteridea to everything final. Everything that contradicts finality speaks with insistence there. Becoming and struggling, the constant preoccupation with the path and the future, with duty and destiny—this constant *tension* is what is asserted to be the meaning of life, the life of the world and of man. It is in this that the soul conceives its essence. It conceives it in a double experience: that of creation and that of the commandment.

Man here experiences the fact that he belongs to an infinity. Infinity besets him whether he goes into himself or beyond himself. He lives in a space without end, part of it, in a time without conclusion, a piece of it. Space and time here both derive from the one, omnipresent, and eternal God. World and eternity are one word, they signify the same infinity. In this infinity, on it, man lives. His realm is the opposite of the merely circumscribed and delimited place, his day is the opposite of a fixed and unchanging fate; his realm is a beyond that points off into the distance, his day is the direction that leads away into the wide expanse. Everything that has been and is given becomes a path to the beyond and the future, to the world beyond and the coming day. All creation is revelation, all past becomes the future. The revelation and the future on their endless path, life in its constant going forward, in its constant inconclusiveness, have been discovered here. All experience is here experience of the infinite, of the tension out of which the finite grows.

Man does not see himself face to face with infinity, but sees himself in it and it in him. He experiences it as encompassing his life, the strength of his life, as his horizon, as an omnipresence. For Plato, the transcendent was something isolated, something separated in the beyond; here it is also a beyond, but one that enters man and grows out of him. God, the Holy One, the Other Being, created everything, and He acts and reveals Himself in everything. Everything is in the tension between the infinite and the given, between the world beyond and this world, between the being other and the being one. It is as though there were a constant struggle between proximity and distance, between becoming and being, between temporal beginning and eternal end. The distance remains—the distance between the finite and the infinite, between the created and the Creator, between man and God; but it is, so to speak, an elastic distance, it becomes a dynamic, kinetic element in the world. Energy replaces art—it is no accident that the Bible condemns the image; it is a thing too fixed and final. God is neither artist nor architect, as in Greek antiquity, he is the living God, the Creator, who for that reason must not be confined in any temple, and of whom it is not permitted to make an image or a work of art, or even to have an idea, of whom it is not permitted to make anything resembling the Greek idol.

In this tension world and life are significant as the creation of the eternal, the revelation of the infinite, the realization of divine power. And this tension begets tension, for all energy begets energy. Nothing is fixed. In the words of an old Jewish saying: "God creates in order to continue to create." This was the interpretation of the third verse in the second chapter of Genesis, which speaks of "His work which God in creating had made." All creation has an élan, it is in constant birth. Creation and revelation, becoming and become, belong together, they condition one another. The universe with all the life in it is caught in the tension between these two elements. The world is neither pure fate nor a pure nature upon which man is de-

138

pendent, nor is it purely the image of an arch-image that man is supposed only to contemplate and adore. It is God's world, an earthly world and yet God's domain, space yet infinity, time yet eternity—or, again to quote an old Jewish saying: "God is the space of the world, but the world is not His space," [1] and it may be added: He is the time of the world, but the world is not His time. The world is the creation and the revelation of God, and therefore a world full of tension. It is characterized both by distance from God and belonging to God. It is the unity of oppositions, an immanence of transcendence, a being-one with being-other, the synthesis of the finite and temporal with the infinite and eternal. In religious emotion both become one, the stream flows between the poles. Man is surrounded by end-less space and endless time, but they neither crush him nor allow him to become absorbed in himself. He has not only the "taste of infinity" and is not only "absolutely dependent," he is also tension towards the infinite—unity in opposition, op-position in unity.

Man experiences this in the world in which he lives as well as in the world that he creates, in his deeds which constitute that world of which a talmudic hyperbole says that "it is greater even than the creation of heaven and earth." In every act that is demanded of him, man experiences the command-ment, and this, too, is the experience of infinity. The command-ment for man is God's commandment, born of the infinite and eternal depth, full of divine restlessness and sacred movement. Every duty to which he is summoned begets a new duty; what-ever he accomplishes is only a step on his way, a step that must be followed by other steps, a step that always has its goal, but never attains its end. He is never finished, his peace is never the peace of final fulfilment. In every commandment that he carries out, he is possessed by God's absoluteness and eternity, by the tension between the finite here below and the infinite beyond. However determined and limited his life, the imperative is unlimited, ultimately it lives in the absolute, in the constantly unfulfilled, it is never past, but always future, it is always renewed. Here, too, there is nothing final, nothing completed, nothing perfect in the life of man; in his action, too, he is surrounded by infinity, it irrupts into him, and his path leads to it. Every commandment is a force that tends to become force. Just as God creates to continue creating, so he commands to continue commanding. The pious man, as the Talmud says, is a man "without rest here or in the beyond." [2]

Thus tension is present in the realm of man's tasks, it acquires activity, an imperative, urgent character, a moral yearning, it becomes the ordained tension. The experience of the infinite becomes the will to the infinite, a duty, a destination given it; it becomes the path of life. God demands the infinite of the finite. At the point where this decision for the infinite takes place, the ethical begins; it dwells where man seeks to possess his life in this infinity, in this always inadequate fulfilment of the commandment, in the holy. The ethical is the categorical, infinite commandment: "Ye shall be holy; for I the Lord your God am holy" (Lev. 19:2); this is the commandment which contains all the other commandments; everything else is only teaching, exhortation and advice. The infinity of man's task was discovered here—the ethics of infinity before the mathematics of infinity, the incomplete and never-completed, which are not the expression of weakness and deficiency, but the revelation of the demanding force, the epiphany of the infinite imperative in the finite, of the divine in the human—

140

not the "sigh of the creature," but the upward-reaching will in him.

Man now desires infinity; he realizes it. He, the finite, who has come forth from infinity and eternity, now is active within it. In every moral act that he accomplishes he helps to create it. He is determined, but determined by God, and all determination by God is in ethics a commandment of him, an indicated direction towards infinity; man has been created, but created by God, and what God creates, morality summons back to Him in order to find its goal in Him. The cause of man is here his goal. His life is God's creation, the polarity, the tension between the here below and the beyond, between this being and the other being. Now creation becomes the task, polarity becomes the destination; the beyond is to become the here below, the other being this being, the kingdom of God the domain of man. There exists in this world the great commandment that enjoins free interaction between the finite and the infinite.

Thus tension ceases to be mere experience of tension. Experience becomes life, creating and begetting; tension becomes the struggle each day exacts. Inherent in this will to infinity is the struggle for it, the struggle with the eternal. The creature struggles with the Creator, man with his God; he struggles for God's commandment and therein achieves his own creativeness, becoming a creator himself. He masters infinity by absorbing it in his will, by living it, by introducing it into his life, by making God's commandments an inner acquisition. He brings the beyond down to this world, he brings it down from heaven to earth, he conquers it and thus "conquers" God, as it were, he makes God come closer and closer to this world. This formulation may sound blasphemous but it is to be found in the Talmud: "God says: My children have prevailed over me." [3] All moral heroism, as well as all moral patience, is in this struggle with the infinite. Mankind took a step forward when one man allowed infinity to enter his life, when he, to reiterate our formulation, "conquered" God. It is a victory that signified the overcoming of the tension, that creates life out of the tension. It is the greatest victory in human life—the victory of the ethical element, the creative element of the Ethos and the Logos and the Eros that man bears within himself.

This victory is the reconciliation and fulfilment of religion —its peace. Man reconciles the finitude of his life with infinity, the temporal with the eternal, the relative with the absolute. To quote another old Jewish saying: "He achieves his eternity and infinity through one hour." [4] Redemption is release from will and therefore from the commandment; reconciliation is reconciliation through the commandment. The redeemed believer is absorbed into infinity; the reconciled believer has mastered it. By accepting it he has brought harmony out of tension. It is seemingly a victory of man over God and yet at the same time in reality a victory of God: God's kingdom extends its domain to earth. It is the reconciliation of man with God and of God with man. "I will not let thee go, except thou bless me"; such is the expression of the reconciliation.

An element of reconciliation is inherent in this tension in another sense. The notion of finality has a dogmatic force, it is conclusive and thereby exclusive. Whatever is fixed and final is intolerant, and whatever belongs merely to the past is intolerant. But the notion of tension is space-creating and time-renewing, it introduces the yearning for the future, for the paths towards the goal, it extends the domain of searching. It is for the infinite that so many struggles are fought, its drama is everywhere, it has its epochs; the absolute finds its tension in the relative. There is room here for individuals and nations. All reconciliation is reconciliation of the tension between the finite and the infinite; and man and nation can reconcile their world on this earth with the one beyond; they can find their proper mode of solution. Where only what is fixed and final constitutes the truth, the principle of unity without exception is dominant—Plato is the initiator of this principle—the principle of the monolithic faith and the monolithic state, and there man experiences the strong and gratifying feeling of *quod semper, quod ubique et ab omnibus*—that holy rest. Where tension is experienced as the meaning of life and is lived as life's commandment, there the will to history begins—and all history is in the last analysis many-sidedness, interaction, and struggle—there history with all the sacred unrest that constitutes its life begins to function. It is at this point that nations enter infinity and it is at this point that reconciliation is given to them, reconciliation in the great tension that is called world history.

Thus there are two ideational forces opposed to one another, a dual type of discovering and knowing that is given to the human spirit. There is that consummated world in which man experiences completion, being, existence as work of art, in which he finds his redemption, his goal and his rest, his ultimate desire, the peace of the temple encompassing him, the trance of adoration, rapture and contemplation—the world of the cult and the great temple. And there is also the world of tension in which man experiences the urge towards the infinite and in which he comprehends his life, where he finds his struggle and his path, the struggle with the commandment and the path towards the commandment, and discovers the day of reconciliation and the covenant with God—the world as the great and revelatory drama of creation. Each of these forces has its own world, its own sanctuary, its own experience.

To which of these two will the future belong? Every thoughtful and observant man, and no doubt every thoughtful and observant nation, has his own eye with which to regard his neighbor and also the future. There are old eyes in which we can read a millenial experience and life, and there are young eyes which imagine that the years they have seen are centuries. There is moral memory and moral inexperience, there is recollection and there is oblivion. When nations and communities do not understand one another, the reason is often that some look at the world in the light of experience, while others question it only in the light of the present. He who wants to grasp the future, the direction of the path, must attempt to see with eyes that are thousands of years old.

It is true that the perfected bears in it the guaranty of duration, it stands firm once it has been erected, it is built for the ages. Its very essence is a will to survive, to possess, and to dominate; its power consists in its ability to possess, dominate, and subject. It can be the consummated faith, the consummated dogma, the consummated state. It can offer what is always the same, perfection itself, to generation after generation. Century after century can turn to it to contemplate what is permanent and to rejoice in what is complete and final. But when the world of finality and perfection once totters, when it once collapses, it is forever broken. When it no longer possesses and no longer rules, it has ended; it has no becoming and therefore no returning. When finality dies, its death is final.

In tension there is no possession. It cannot subject and

144

dominate; it can only realize and re-create. Therefore it can be reborn. He who experiences the infinite and eternal through his life, experiences it endlessly and without conclusion; he who struggles with it wages the fight that is continually recommenced, that is always new, and he himself is perpetually renewed in it. He does not see God but he sees the path towards Him, the path of the eternal commandment, the never-ending journey that God demands of man. Every day on this path man struggles with the commandment, is often wearied but then triumphs nevertheless, and in this struggle he is reconciled, renewed and reborn again and again. There is neither end nor conclusion to the reconciliation. Every tension has its renaissance. In it there is no permanent rest, but there is no death, either. The religion of tension, the culture that lives in it, cannot die. It can be pressed down to the ground, it can grow weary, it can slumber—but it cannot die, it is always reborn. And only he is reborn who experiences this tension and struggles with it, who bears in himself the knowledge of infinity and the will to it, who knows that his own life was created by God and should itself create for God—that it is there in order to build a kingdom of God in an earthly existence.

THE CHARACTER OF JUDAISM

THE CHARACTER OF JUDAISM

To possess a special genius, to express one's soul in an individual way, also means to be different, set apart from, and opposed to the surrounding world. Real originality always stands in opposition to its milieu and time. There is always involved in it this choice: either passively withdrawing from the world, or struggling actively and continually against it everywhere in order to convince it and convert it. The man with a soul of his own is either a hermit or an apostle. The hermit turns only to himself, the apostle to the future. Thus real originality may exist in either a dynamic or a static form which is independent of place or fate and denotes an essential difference and a definite character. While one man plays an active role in the world and remains a hermit nevertheless, another, although he may live under the most restricted circumstances, is an apostle and a missionary, without intending it perhaps, or even against his own will.

In the beginning, originality of spirit always manifests itself in an individual personality, in a single man with a highly evolved individuality. If it is of the dynamic kind, it can take possession of a whole group predisposed to it, and in the end, a whole nation, pervading it, shaping it, and marking it irrevocably. And thus this nation acquires a specific genius—a historical personality. The historical personality, whether it is that of an individual or a nation, has an element of particularity, since it is distinguished and separated from the many, but it also has an element of universality, in that it turns against the world and thus appeals to it—its particularity exists for the sake of the universal. This relation of the particular to the universal is the characteristic feature of dynamic individuality and is responsible for the creation of the historical personality.

The people of Judaism, the Jewish people, is a particular example—perhaps the most striking example—of such dynamic personality. The national character of no other nation can wholly be compared with it. It is almost as if it is a word that the Creator pronounced for one time only. The strength of the Jewish genius is such that it could and can exist only in a small community or nation. It was created by great religious personalities, and through them it later became the possession of a whole nation. And since possession is at the same time an obligation, particularity has become this nation's task; one might almost say that this particularity is its historical vocation. The dynamic genius lives in this nation and has made it into a historical personality, full of the particular and the universal at the same time, and the nation lives by this genius.

The powers that Judaism opposed and whose victory it denied often isolated it in order to hinder and check its dynamism. And sometimes this nation itself, fully aware of the opposition but weary of the struggle, wanted to bring its dynamism to a rest and transform it into a static quality, and so accepted isolation of itself. But the dynamism was too strong and always broke through again. Time and again Judaism reassumed its character as a motive force, and it has remained that—a ferment in the history of the spirit, a leaven in the history of the human will.

Therefore Judaism has a twofold history. First, it has an internal history, a history within the people of Judaism that is revealed in the fact that its specific genius has repeatedly become aware of itself, or, what amounts to the same thing, has repeatedly and ever anew sought and found its own means of expression. Second, it has an external history, the history that passed beyond the confines of this nation and had its time and place outside of it. This other history is revealed in the repeated penetration of the genius of Judaism into the world, in its activity in the world and in the world's reaction to it. One is the history of the struggle that Judaism has waged for itself —and sometimes against itself; the other, that of the struggle that it has waged for and against the world. There is no spiritual dynamism without struggle.

Judaism is dynamic above all because it entered the domain of human thought as a revolution. It originated in a revolution, perhaps the most radical that man's spirit has ever experienced. A spiritual revolution—and every true political revolution can also be referred back to a spiritual one—is the postulation of an entirely new principle, the assumption of an entirely new point of view. It is an absolutely new beginning. It demands a break with the past and with everything that was valid before it. It is a new creation—not simply the result of a growth. Therefore it is not the perfecting or the refinement or the last consequence of an old principle—all this would have been only an evolution. Nor is it an attempt to connect something new with the old, to adjust the old to the new—that would be only a reform or compromise. It is rather something unconditionally new—the unconditional abandonment of the previous path, the unconditional negation of the previous direction. It rejects absolutely in order to be able to demand absolutely.

True revolutions, revolutions in the world of the spirit, are extremely rare. They are the turning points of time, the deepest incursions into history; with them new epochs begin. Yet only in the light of these revolutions are the course and meaning of history understandable. History cannot be regarded as only evolution, however much such an approach may be justified with regard to single periods. It is the defect of Hegel's historical method that it overlooks or ignores the crucial factor of revolution. Hegel's conception of history as proceeding by thesis, antithesis, and synthesis may be correct for non-revolutionary periods, which often last a long time. In such periods opposition and compromise, reaction and reform, have their place and their uses. But when a revolution flares up and formulates its new principle, there arises the demand to turn one's back upon every road that has been followed. Every synthesis, every play between thesis and antithesis, is now rejected. Only one thing is valid—the new principle, the new path. It was as such a revolution, at first unnoticed by the world and then profoundly felt by it, that Judaism entered history and set it on a new path.

This revolution has a character and dynamism entirely its own not only because the new principle contained in it expresses a new and entirely different idea, but also because it expresses a new and entirely different task with which man is confronted. No matter how revolutionary an idea and no matter how clearly it establishes its new principle, it yet contains a conclusion within itself, an end as well as a beginning; it announces something final and definitive; it is fulfilment in itself. But the human task is never completed, for it refers not only to what is and has been established, but also to what should be and what is still to be accomplished. Every task sees the future before it. Moreover, the dynamic new principle is in this instance an ethical one, hence the task concerns mankind in all the conditions and days of its life, it concerns all mankind and its history. The word that is constantly repeated here is the word "whole" or "all"—"the whole commandment," "all the commandments," "with all thy heart, and with all thy soul, and with all thy might," "all peoples," "all nations," "and it shall come to pass in the end of days."

Ethics, too, has this twofold character, static and dynamic. The former encourages an equilibrium in man and among men, and it is therefore above everything else a utilitarian ethics; it preaches that which conduces towards equilibrium and compromise. It seeks, so to speak, to distribute the weight to both scales in an equitable fashion. The other, the dynamic ethics, postulates a single point of view, a single position, a single direction; it makes an unconditional demand, it admits of only one decisive weight. It is able—and often is fated—to reject every "now" and to demand the new day. It bids us measure each present moment against the ultimate goal, every existing condition against the highest conception of value. This dynamic ethics is therefore messianic. It will not be realized until the whole imperative in its full force is fulfilled by all men. And by virtue of its nature this dynamic ethics always remains messianic. Ethics and messianism both, they constitute a unity here; there is no ethics without the messianic element, and no messianism without the ethical element. There is no goal and no salvation without the fulfilment of the commandment.

Every revolution embodies a problem. Every revolution

153

embodies one of those great queries that humanity puts to itself. It can be one of those great but partial questions, of a scientific, artistic, political, or social character, or it can be one of those comprehensive questions that pertains to the whole of man and his soul; perhaps that one great question whose essence contains all the other questions. There are only a few problems that mankind has struggled with constantly since it has begun to think. Each of these problems has recurred many times since it was first raised, and each recurrence constituted a rebirth of the spirit, a rebirth of mankind. The history of the spirit is a history of renaissances. The nature of a real revolution is such that it is destined to be reborn. Once it was new, and it becomes new over and over again. At one time it was possible to call it old; and yet now it must be called new.

Small minds desirous of depreciating greatness, and great minds that have conceived the great in all its abiding greatness, have often come across this old-in-new, however different their motivation and insight. When modern philosophy was initiated under Descartes and Spinoza, their adversaries wrote works entitled *Cartesiani ante Cartesium* and *Spinozistae ante Spinozam*—Cartesians before Descartes, and Spinozists before Spinoza; they tried to show that the ideas of these thinkers had been discovered by others at an earlier date. When Kant's theory revolutionized philosophy, Schopenhauer strove to show that Plato had already taught the same thing. When Hegel's philosophy stirred the world, Ferdinand Lassalle wrote his book, *The Philosophy of Heraclitus the Obscure*, in which he sought to prove that Hegel's ideas had already been set forth by this ancient Greek thinker. The problem was the same, in fact, in both cases—the old problem that had once been new became new again. This is at bottom the meaning of Goethe's

154

well-known maxim that all wisdom has been thought of before, and that one must only try to think it again. It is the history of the rebirths of the few great problems of humanity.

The problem that passed into the consciousness of mankind with the religion and spirit of Israel, and that since then has not been absent from the mind, will, and deepest strivings of man, has manifested and expressed itself in a variety of ways, but is one in its essential nature. Creative personalities have experienced and discovered the invisible world of the One, of the Existing, of the Eternal and Infinite. This world creatively irrupted into the visible world of finiteness, transience, and change, and constantly irrupts into it. This creative world is also the world of the Holy, the Ordaining, and the Promising. This world of the Existing, of the Creative, and the Holy, created and ordered everything that exists, all life, and especially human life, and gave human life its destiny. Thus the problem has a fourfold form, but its root is one; it is the problem of life with regard to what it is and what it ought to be. This problem, as embodied in the religion of Israel, took hold of man, releasing a revolutionary dynamism in him and acting as a ferment and motive force in his innermost being.

Men realized that behind, beneath, or above everything that exists, there is something else—the One, creative, ordaining, ordering. Everything that exists, therefore, has not only existence, but also meaning; for meaning is revealed when, behind, beneath or above the compound and the manifold, man perceives the oneness—when the thinker discovers the idea behind the phenomena, when the scientist discovers the law behind the sequence of facts, when the artist discovers the essence or soul behind the visible surface—when all of them discover something of which the thing that they see, hear, or feel is only a manifestation. And these men, who were imbued with the spirit of Israel, conceived the whole unity that is behind, above, and beneath everything that is one, which is the first and ultimate unity, and they conceived it as the one force, the eternal, infinite, all-creating force from which come all commandments, all promises and all certainties.

The principle thus established was clear and immutable. Everything emanates from the One, from the only Being. Creation and commandment, life and ethics, both have the same origin and arise from the same root. Therefore each and every thing can be understood only if related to and understood as a part of the One. Man has the correct point of view only if he judges on the basis of the One. Starting here, he arrives at the truth and attains certainty, learns to understand the commandment which then becomes his task, and learns to understand the life that has been given him. Starting here, he is able to realize that the life of man is at the same time his task, and that the task of man is his life, and that his life and his task are fulfilled only if all the ways of his doing, thinking, and hoping are ways emanating from the One and leading to it. This is the principle that is revealed here; this is the yardstick by which to measure everything.

When man discovered this and thought it through for the first time and strove to give it expression—for in man all thinking is also speaking—it could naturally be expressed only in the language that was at hand. The new thought had to speak with the old words. All new thinking is therefore also a struggle with the word, a struggle for expression. Such a struggle was waged here, and here, too, something revolutionary resulted. Many words now acquired a new and dynamic content whose effectiveness in moving and stirring people was

156

continually renewed and extended. Whenever a new idea is expressed, words are at first only a kind of bridge over which one passes to the idea. Here, where the new principle had to be expressed, where words were intended to lead to a new and hitherto unknown land, the words themselves—the old words with a new content—represented a way that had to be paved, a new way that was now supposed to be entered upon. Here words became a kind of task, a power with a duty attached to it, and in this consists their history.

Above all, the word "God" now acquired a completely new and different meaning; it now acquired its strength and dynamism. If only by virtue of its majestic singular, it was bound to signify something that had never been expressed in any other language. But, above all, it now became the expression of the new principle. It expressed the primary and ultimate unity that is the creative power in which everything originates, the foundation of all moral law, the guarantee of all certainty, the source of man's values, goals, tasks. The word "God" is now something new and unique to which nothing else can be compared. So strong was this new idea that the ancient Hebrews created a new word for it, a word that is untranslatable since it exists only in that language and that had to be explained even in the language that had created it. It is explained as "I am that I am"—the I of all I's, the Being of all Beings. It is the new revelation through the new, revolutionary, and dynamic word. With it a new era begins.

What followed was a general transformation of the content of the language. The old words became a new language, a language of humanity. And with it this revolutionary element entered into mankind. One perceives two worlds of language when the meaning such words as commandment, justice, love,

157

help, way, brother, fellow man, poor, foreigner, beast, rest, honor, joy, comfort, peace, and future have among the Hebrews by virtue of the new principle is compared with their meaning everywhere else. We can imagine what a revolution was accomplished when the one world came into contact with the other and began to penetrate it step by step. The ways of this dynamic language were an essential part of the history of the dynamic spirit of Judaism. In it, this spirit possessed an effective instrument that opened the way to it to the rest of mankind.

This language created a book of a distinctive character. This book perhaps comprises only part of many writings of the same kind that were created by the Jewish people—we do not know how much was lost in the catastrophe of the Babylonian Exile. But just as this people, by virtue of the dynamism of its spirit and its distinctive character, not only survived, but also overcame this and later catastrophes, so its language retained its vitality and its classical writings survived a destruction that was directed against life itself. That book into which several books were combined is one of absolute originality. People were very early conscious of its uniqueness, so much so that they called it the Book. And it is, in fact, a book of humanity and man's revolution, as hardly any other book is.

It is a book so full of dynamism that both within and without the Jewish nation it has repeatedly compelled people to take a stand with regard to it. It presented man with a certainty that could set his mind at rest and yet at the same time has never let him rest. People who made this book their own could never realize what had been given them without experiencing all that the book demanded of them. And just as it is a book of exhortations and commandments, so is it also a book of questions.

What it says will never be obsolete. Men have learned over and over again from it the true meaning of new knowledge and new tasks. The "Written Law" has been repeatedly supplemented by the "Oral Law," and it, too, was the teaching of this book. There was no one road but only the many roads by whose ways each age and place could approach this book. The internal and external history of Judaism is also the history of the struggle over this book—and occasionally even against it. Only thus could it be the book it is, the book of dynamism. Had it been a book in which one could have found rest, a static book, its people would have lost it.

The special genius of the Jewish people created this book, and this book, in turn, shaped, strengthened, and preserved the spirit of this people. This spirit was all the more vital and marked because it was intended to embrace all of man and his life. The spirit of Judaism rejected every division of mankind and every division of life. And thus it rejected every division of morality, of law and of hope. It knows and postulates the whole, the unity of man and life. Thus religion is here not a part of man and a part of life, but is that very whole. Piety here is not an affair of particular hours and days, but of every day and all hours. It, too, is dynamic. Thus Judaism denotes a definite kind and way of life, a definite kind and way of humanity, a style of life and a style of humanity that have to be continually renewed and forged again. This style is expressed in all the manifestations and activities of life, in work, and in rest and relaxation, as well. And the way in which man reposes and the kind of holidays he creates are more expressive of his character than his works; his evenings are more expressive of him than his days. Man lives and dies according to the particular quality of his evenings—man, and perhaps an entire people, too.

Dynamic man does not exist apart from a community. For that reason alone the Jewish spirit is the spirit of that will which strives toward the realization of the community. By means of this dynamic spirit there was discovered the fellow man, the poor man, the foreigner, the man who is nothing but a man, and mankind itself. They were discovered as a task set before man. This, too, is the new principle, and here again it means a new point of view, a new way of seeing and hearing. This provides the basis for the giving of the laws, the laws that follow from the new principle and point of view. The point of view is that of the needy, the weak, and the powerless, for in them the as yet imperfect unity that is to be created is clearly recognizable. All justice here is of the positive kind, intended not only to prevent wrong, but to create and produce right. Thus there is no question here of a divided right or different orders of right. There is only the one, whole right—the positive, democratic, social right that follows from the new principle. It is no accident that the classical principle of the new democracy, the principle of what should be done by the people and for the people, was formulated in an introduction to a translation of the Bible, the one made by Wycliff; and that new and powerful social ideas and new and living social doctrines have arisen repeatedly from the spirit of the Jewish people.

Judaism is the life of a unique spirit or, one might also say, it is a unique kind of life. Like everything truly original it has its own secret. Judaism and the dynamism of Judaism have their roots in this secret. Its rationale draws its strength from the irrational. Therefore it can never be refuted—one can only live opposed to it. It can never be fettered, if only because

160

it has no dogmas. It is elastic, like everything dynamic. Its fecundity endures and begets the new again and again. It remains, to borrow a phrase from Leibniz's *Monadologie*, *"gros de l'avenir,"* pregnant with the future. Until "the end of days," it will not reach its end.

Judaism has its history and its history is the history of this special genius. True originality of spirit, when it is as dynamic as that of the Jews, never stands still, and therefore it has a history. It is the history of a law and of a hope, the history of the faith in a way of life. The word "way" is one of the most characteristic words of the Bible, one of the words in which eternity and finitude try to meet—the way of God and the way of man. The mission of a people here is not one of achieving power, but of finding the way. The way is the law that God gives and man heeds, so that the way of God becomes the way of man and the will of God and the will of man become one.

The history of Judaism has passed beyond the boundaries dividing the Jewish people and Judaism from the rest of the world. Two great historical forms of world religion, a world philosophy, and a world socialism have arisen from it, and they can endure only so long as they remain true to their origin. Wherever they have attempted to negate Judaism, they themselves were negated. Thus certain essential ideas and elements of Judaism have become part of mankind's heritage. One might divide the world of man into two domains: the one, into which something of the power of this spirit has penetrated, and the other, into which it has not, or as yet has not, penetrated.

And amidst all this, the people of Judaism, caught up in the history of every epoch, led and often driven, endures and moves forward, knowing that its life depends upon its faithfulness to

Judaism, and thus to itself. It exists in its particularity, in the singularity of its spirit, of its will and of its trust; it is particular even in the fact that it clings to its old land. It exists in its universality as a people of mankind, like a symbol of mankind, universal even where it has taken deep root in a particular soil.

NOTES

THE PHARISEES: [1] Sifra, Lev. 19:2 (ed. Weiss), 86c. [2] *Ibid.*, 20:26, 93d. [3] Mekhilta, Exod. 19:2 (ed. Weiss), 71a. [4] Sifra, Lev. 20:7, 91d. [5] *Ibid.*, 20:26, 93d. [6] Mekhilta S.b.Y., Exod. 19:6 (ed. Hoffmann), 95. [7] Sifra, Lev. 20:7, 91d. [8] Sifre, Num. 15:40 (ed. Friedmann), 35a. [9] Mekhilta S.b.Y., Exod. 19:6, 95. [10] *Bel. Jud.* ii. 18. 7. [11] Shabbat 14b. [12] *Ibid.*, 15a, and Avodah Zarah 8b. [13] Yer. Maaser Sheni 53d. [14] Avot I, 1. [15] *Antt.* xiii. 10. 6. [16] *Ibid.* [17] *Ibid.*, xvii. 2. 4. [18] *Bel. Jud.* i. 5. 2. [19] *Vita* 38. [20] *Bel. Jud.* ii. 8. 14. [21] Sifre, Deut. 11:13, 80a. [22] *Ibid.* [23] *Ibid.*, 13:5, 92a. [24] Sifre Zutta, Num. 18:4 (ed. Horowitz), 292. [25] Sifre, Deut. 11:13, 80a. [26] Targum, Deut. 13:5. [27] Baba Kamma 92b, and Baba Metzia 107b. [28] Yer. Berakhot 8b. [29] Sifre, Num. 6:27 (ed. Friedmann), 13b. [30] *See* Mal. 2:7. [31] Sifre, Num. 18:20 (ed. Friedmann), 40a. [32] *Antt.* xx. 11. 2. [33] Yer. Berakhot, Deut. 17:11, 3b. [34] Baba Metzia, Deut. 30:12, 59b. [35] Avot III, 16. [36] Shabbat 12b.

TRADITION IN JUDAISM: [1] Avot II, 17. [2] Sanhedrin 90b. [3] Avot V, 25.

JUDAISM IN THE CHURCH: [1] Sanhedrin 97a; cf. Yer. Megillah 70d. [2] Niddah 61b; Pesahim 50a; Shabbat 151b; Yalkut Shimeoni to Isaiah 26:2. [3] Tertullian *Adversus Marcionem* I, 29. [4] *Ibid.*, I, 14. [5] Cf. I Cor. 6:12 *et seq.*, and 8:7 *et seq.*; I Pet. 2:16. [6] Epiphanius *Panarion* 39. [7] *Catechismus Romanus* VII, 23. [8] Cf. the words of Amsdorf, an assistant of Luther's, in Hase, *Hutterus redivivus: "Bona opera ad salutem esse perniciosa."*

THE ORIGIN OF JEWISH MYSTICISM: [1] The same text contains other words of praise by Yohanan, probably from another tradition: "Many preach nobly and do not act nobly; many act nobly and do not preach nobly; Eleazar ben Arakh both preaches and acts nobly. Be praised, our father Abraham, that Eleazar ben Arakh is descended of you!" What is significant here is the affirmation of the unity of ethics and mysticism, study and action. Two other disciples of Yohanan are then promised the world to come as a reward for their mystical knowledge. [2] The turning away from Hellenism—and so from Gnosticism—that took place after the Bar Kokhba rebellion was a contributing factor. The repudiation of large parts of the apocryphal literature, which deals with *Maaseh Bereshit* and the *Merkavah*, was doubtless connected with this development. [3] The context of this passage (Yer. Hagigah 77a) indicates that this is its meaning. [4] Teshuvot ha-Geonim, Lyck, No. 99, p. 31.

GREEK AND JEWISH PREACHING: [1] Jacob Freudenthal, *Die Flavius Josephus beigelegte Schrift über die Herrschaft der Vernunft* (Breslau, 1869), p. 4 *et seq.* [2] Lysias *Against Andocides: For Impiety.* [3] *See* the Act of the Apostles, 18:4; 19:8-9; 20:9; 24:25. In each of the passages the word διαλέγεσθαι is used in the sense of "to preach." [4] Philo *De special. leg.* i. (*De monarchia*). [5] Genesis Rabbah 44.14. [6] Plato *Phaedrus* (Jowett translation). [7] Genesis Rabbah, *loc. cit.* [8] Shabbat 156a. [9] Genesis Rabbah 17.5 and 44.17. [10] Midrash Tehillim 17.8.

TWO WORLD VIEWS COMPARED: [1] Genesis Rabbah 68.10. [2] Berakhot 64a. [3] Baba Metzia 59b. [4] Avodah Zarah 10b.

KANSAS SCHOOL OF RELIGION
University of Kansas
1300 Oread Avenue
LAWRENCE, KANSAS 66044

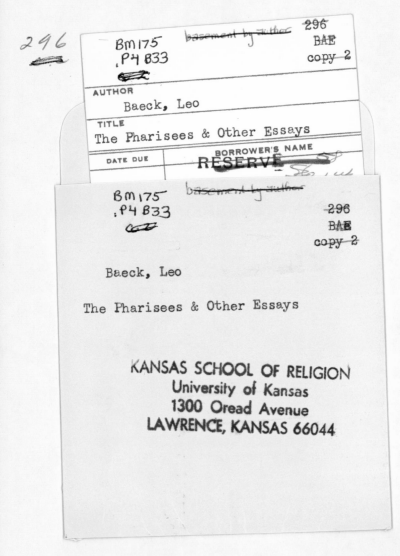

296

BM175
.P4 B33

basement by author

296
BAE
copy 2

AUTHOR
Baeck, Leo

TITLE
The Pharisees & Other Essays

DATE DUE | BORROWER'S NAME
RESERVE

BM175
.P4 B33

basement by author

296
BAE
copy 2

Baeck, Leo

The Pharisees & Other Essays

KANSAS SCHOOL OF RELIGION
University of Kansas
1300 Oread Avenue
LAWRENCE, KANSAS 66044